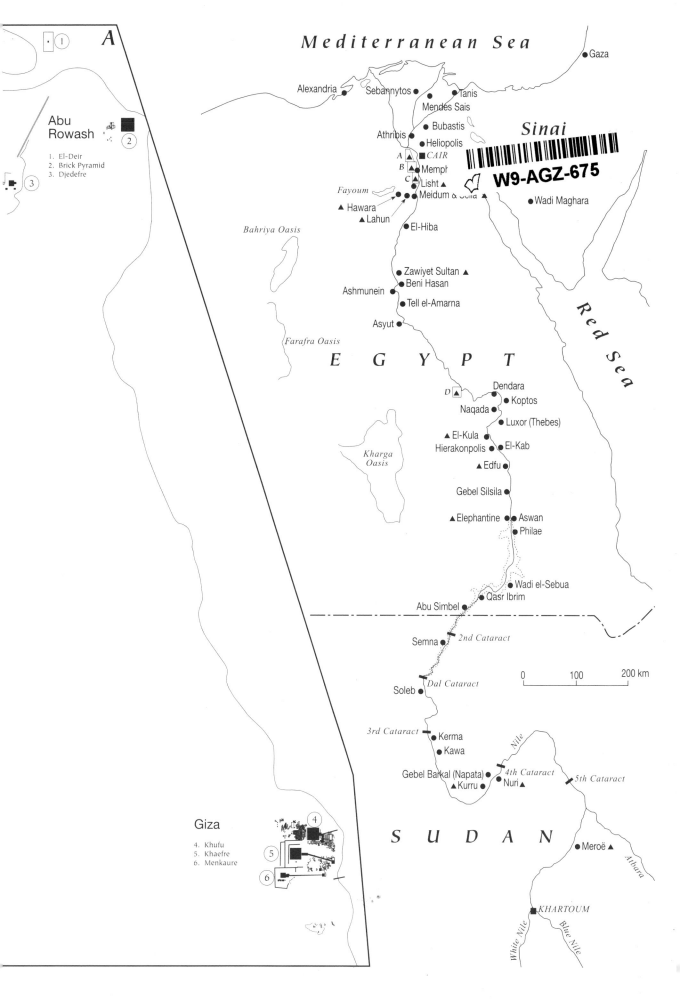

Mediterranean Sea

Gaza

Alexandria
Sebennytos
Tanis
Mendes Sais
Bubastis
Athribis
Heliopolis
A ▲ *CAIR*
B ▲ Memphis
C ▲ Lisht ▲
Fayoum
Meidum & Dahshur ▲
▲ Hawara
▲ Lahun
El-Hiba

Zawiyet Sultan ▲
Beni Hasan
Ashmunein
Tell el-Amarna
Asyut

E G Y P T

D ▲
Dendara
Koptos
Naqada
Luxor (Thebes)
▲ El-Kula
Hierakonpolis
El-Kab
▲ Edfu
Gebel Silsila
▲ Elephantine
Aswan
Philae

Wadi el-Sebua
Abu Simbel
Qasr Ibrim

Semna
2nd Cataract

Soleb
Dal Cataract

3rd Cataract
Kerma
Kawa
Gebel Barkal (Napata)
4th Cataract
5th Cataract
Kurru
Nuri ▲

S U D A N

Meroë ▲

KHARTOUM

Sinai

Red Sea

Wadi Maghara

Bahriya Oasis

Farafra Oasis

Kharga Oasis

Nile

Athara

White Nile

Blue Nile

A

Abu
Rowash

1. El-Deir
2. Brick Pyramid
3. Djedefre

1
2
3

Giza

4. Khufu
5. Khaefre
6. Menkaure

4
5
6

0   100   200 km

THE
PYRAMIDS
OF ANCIENT EGYPT

THE
PYRAMIDS
OF ANCIENT EGYPT

AIDAN DODSON

NEW HOLLAND

First published in 2003 by New Holland Publishers (UK) Ltd
London • Cape Town • Sydney • Auckland

2 4 6 8 10 9 7 5 3 1

www.newhollandpublishers.com

Garfield House, 86–88 Edgware Road, London W2 2EA, United
Kingdom

80 McKenzie Street, Cape Town 8001, South Africa

14 Aquatic Drive, Frenchs Forest, NSW 2086, Australia

218 Lake Road, Northcote, Auckland, New Zealand

ISBN 1 84330 495 3

Publishing Manager: Jo Hemmings
Senior Editor: Kate Michell
Assistant Editor: Rose Hudson
Design & cover design: Alan Marshall
Production: Joan Woodroffe
Cartography: William Smuts
Index: Richard Bird

Reproduction by Pica Digital Pte Ltd, Singapore
Printed and bound in Singapore by Star Standard Industries (Pte) Ltd

Half title page: King Menkauhor, as shown in an Eighteenth Dynasty
relief from the tomb of Amenemonet at Saqqara; title page: Khaefre's
pyramid and the Sphinx at Giza; page 4: Statue of Khaefre; page 5 (top):
The Step Pyramid at Saqqara, (middle) The Bent Pyramid at Dahshur,
(bottom) The pyramid of Senwosret II at Lahun.

CONTENTS

PREFACE

Why another book on pyramids? Over the past few years, booksellers' shelves have been groaning under the weight of books dealing with, or related to, Egypt's pyramids; but a closer inspection shows that many – if not most – are not concerned with their reality, a matter to which I will return. Of the remainder, although including some very fine works, none provides an authoritative, yet simple, up-to-date listing of *all* known examples belonging to kings and queens of Egypt. It is this gap that I have set out to fill, by providing an accessible, well-illustrated handbook for the use of anyone interested in these stupendous monuments.

Being 'up to date' isn't easy. Just as I was about to key these words, a news report informed me that a 'new' queen's pyramid had been found at Abu Rowash. Barely a week earlier, a report at a conference I was attending showed that a key piece of 'evidence', revealed only a few years ago, had been found actually to be something completely different; as a result, a number of paragraphs had to be reworked. Such is the pace of archaeology in Egypt at the moment that one's work is liable to be current only until the moment the text is out of one's hands!

However desirable, and difficult, it is to be up to date, the wisdom received from one's Egyptological forebears is no less valuable, and it is certainly not the case that all 'new' ideas will come to replace the 'old'; what matters is what best fits all the evidence, from whatever direction it comes. Failure to comprehend the whole wide body of evidence that now exists is what damns the large body of literature on the pyramids that, as I briefly noted above, has only tenuous links with reality. These are the tomes concerned with weaving gossamer-thin theories according to which the pyramids – or at least the best-known ones, at Giza – were built or inspired by a very ancient lost civilization (usually Atlanteans or extra-terrestrials, though you can insert your group of choice and someone will have thought of it). As to the pyramids' purpose (or at least, that of the biggest one at Giza), a mind-boggling variety of suggestions are advanced: navigation beacons for spaceships, initiation centres (masonic or otherwise), energy-generation devices, observatories and repositories for esoteric knowledge (whether or not crystal-encoded) are a random selection.

Overwhelming evidence in favour of the pyramids being simply the tombs of the kings of Egypt between around 2700 and 1500 BC has so far failed to stem the flow. This may be in part because the archaeological 'establishment' has often been insufficiently willing to engage with the 'fringe' out of a sense of its being beneath them to do so. On the other hand, the practitioners of 'alternative archaeology' (their own term) are generally so far outside the bounds of scientific reasoning as to make meaningful discourse between the two groups distinctly problematic. However, a number of television documentaries are now challenging certain of these alternative theories head-on – although the very same television stations are not infrequently continuing to promote these very theories through other productions! In addition, an excellent book (Lawton and Ogilvie-Herald, 1999) – a work all the more effective in coming from outside the allegedly 'tainted' world of

'establishment' Egyptian archaeology – has now undertaken a systematic demolition of a number of the key mantras of the 'alternative' camp.

It is against this background that I present this book as a digest of the key facts about the pyramids. I also hope that the photographs, many of them not seen before, and including some of even the most obscure examples, will show something of the majesty inherent in even the most ruined of these outstanding monuments, framed by the golden sand and azure sky of Egypt.

Aidan Dodson
Department of Archaeology,
University of Bristol

Explanatory Notes

This book is intended to cover all pyramids built by the kings and queens of Egypt, but not the large number subsequently erected by private individuals. In additon, a number of related monuments that fit into the developmental sequence of the pyramid complex, although without a truly pyramidal central feature, are included. Thus, every known king's tomb from the Third Dynasty to the opening of the Eighteenth Dynasty is covered.

For each monument the same basic data is provided, insofar as it is available. This comprises the ancient and modern designation(s) of the monument; its date; its owner; the evidence upon which this attribution is based; and the designed dimensions of the pyramid itself, insofar as they can be reconstructed from its current state. The text describes the salient features of the pyramid and its complex, highlighting the explorations of the monument in the modern era.

It may be noted that many pyramids and tombs have been given numbers or letters; royal examples are set out on pages 140–41. A large number were catalogued by Carl Richard Lepsius in the 1840s – these are the Roman numerals prefixed with the letter 'L.'. Other prefixes are used for other tombs, and the less obvious ones are included in the glossary.

INTRODUCTION

During the three millennia of Egypt's ancient history, pyramids were used for the burial of kings and queens for just over a thousand years. They varied widely in size and detail, but otherwise fitted into a basic concept for the Egyptian tomb that can be traced from the earliest times.

So what is this ancient and fascinating land that has produced such breathtaking monumental architecture?

Below: The River Nile has been the key to the life of Egypt since time immemorial. From Aswan, the southernmost city of Egypt, the river winds 800 miles (500km) to the sea.

The modern Arab Republic of Egypt (ARE) occupies nearly a million square kilometres of the north-east corner of the African continent. However, only a tiny proportion – four per cent – of the territory is inhabited. A small part of the population lives in the oases of the Western Desert, but the overwhelming majority live in a narrow strip bordering the River Nile. Indeed, the Egypt of old was defined as this strip of land. As the river flows northwards, to travel south is to go up-river: thus southern Egypt is 'Upper' Egypt, while Lower Egypt comprises the Nile delta and the adjoining area around modern Cairo.

Above: Cairo – the largest city in Africa – sprawls for mile upon mile. From the ancient citadel, look through the smog and across Cairene rooftops to glimpse the pyramids of Giza on the opposite side of the city

Upper and Lower Egypt

Upper and Lower Egypt are very different. In the south, the cultivable area varies in width from nothing to a number of miles, beyond which it gives way to low desert that rapidly rises up to the arid plateaux of the Eastern (Arabian) and Western (Libyan) deserts. In contrast, the delta spreads out in a great triangle towards the Mediterranean, with mile upon mile of flat, fertile land, criss-crossed by canals and wholly dissimilar to the southern Nile valley in both appearance and ethos.

Traditionally, the ancient Egyptian state was held to have extended from the shores of the Mediterranean to Aswan; however, at many points in its history it reached much further south into Nubia, encompassing the southern part of the present ARE and the northern part of what is now the Democratic Republic of the Sudan. The lands bordering this section of the Nile, which since the building of the High Dam at Aswan in the 1960s have been swallowed up by the waters of Lake Nasser, were far more barren than those further north, and mainly of interest as a source of raw materials and a trade route to the far south. River-borne communication south of Aswan was hindered by a series of cataracts or rapids, the first just above that city, the sixth and last just below modern Khartoum.

The Gift of the Nile

It has become the ultimate cliché to describe Egypt as the 'gift of the Nile': a phrase coined by the Greek writer Hecetaeus, and almost universally misattributed to his grandson, the famous traveller Herodotus, who visited Egypt around 450 BC. By 'gift of the Nile' Hecetaeus meant that without the river, the country and its civilization would not – could not – have existed in anything like the form that is so well known. For, outside the margins of the river and the handful of oases, the country is desert.

Today, agriculture in Egypt is dependent upon year-round irrigation, made possible by a series of dams built across the river since the beginning of the 20th century. In all the preceding centuries, however, the growing of crops depended on the annual natural inundation of the Nile. In summer, rains in the Ethiopian highlands swell the river's tributaries, the Atbara and Blue Nile; today, this inundation merely restocks Lake Nasser, but in the past it led to the flooding of the entire Nile valley and delta, an inundation given divine personification as Hapy. The waters spread to cover all the agricultural land, and on receding in October–November they left behind a rich layer of fertile silt on the fields. Crops planted in these fields were ready for harvesting in March–April, with little or no watering required in the interim.

Below: Just north of Cairo and many of the pyramids, the Nile valley opens out into the delta. Looking from Abu Rowash towards Cairo, the pyramids of Giza and the green fields of the southern tip of the delta itself are visible on the right and left respectively.

Throughout these centuries, agriculture was the principal occupation of the Egyptian population, based upon small villages dotted up and down the river. The inundation cycle made for a very irregular distribution of work across the year. After the rising of the flood, dykes would have to be maintained to prevent the water from leaving the fields too early, or flooding the villages, and then the crops would have to be sown and, later, harvested. In between these high-points of activity, work was rather easier than under perennial cultivation methods. One consequence of this was that men could more easily be diverted to labour on public works. The fairly low ancient population, ranging from only two million in the New Kingdom (16th–11th centuries BC) to perhaps five million in Roman times (compared with well over 60 million today), meant that agriculture did not need to be particularly intensive to provide for adequate sustenance plus the surplus from which taxes were levied to support the many activities of the state.

The people of Egypt

The population of Egypt has always been racially mixed, its inhabitants ranging in appearance from the light skin-tones of the north to the dark brown of the far south. Further variety and mixing resulted from successive waves of immigration, both peaceful and hostile, particularly into the north-east delta – as witnessed by

the Bible stories of Abraham and Joseph. Thus, by the time of the New Kingdom, Egypt was a cosmopolitan society, with foreign gods worshipped and men of foreign extraction holding senior government and military positions.

Human habitation of the area now called Egypt goes back to Palaeolithic (Old Stone Age) times, when the territory bore little resemblance to its later form: what is now desert was covered in forests and fed by numerous watercourses. Plentiful stone tools survive, particularly from the Middle Palaeolithic era (*c.*100,000–50,000 BC) and later, relating to a hunting, fishing and gathering society.

The dawning of the Neolithic era (New Stone Age), with its adoption of agriculture, seems to have followed on from climatic changes around 7000 BC, producing what are referred to as the Fayoum A and B cultures in Lower Egypt. Separate material cultures flourished in Upper (i.e. southern) Egypt; the first known grouping, the Badarian, appears just before 5000 BC and then develops into the Naqada I (or Amratian: *c.* 4000–3500 BC), Naqada II (or Gerzean: *c.* 3500–3150 BC) and Naqada III (*c.* 3150–3000 BC) cultures, each distinguishable by its forms of pottery and other items. Collectively, they are usually known as the Predynastic Period, although it is now common to spin off Naqada III as the Protodynastic. These cultures are named after the sites where they were first identified – Badari, El-Amra, Gerza and Naqada; Naqada I and II are simply alternative, more modern, terms for the Amratian and Gerzean.

Above: South of Cairo, in the valley, the desert sometimes constricts cultivation to a narrow strip on one or both banks of the Nile. Here, at Beni Hasan, the far (west) bank is by far the more fertile.

Above: The obelisk of Senwosret I is the last surviving standing monument of the city of Heliopolis, the focus of the sun-cult that was so important to the pyramid builders. Pyramids themselves were symbols of the sun's rays striking through the clouds.

By around 3300 BC, the polities of southern Egypt seem to have begun to coalesce into a more substantial grouping, centred on the town of Hierakonpolis. It is here that we find the first known traces of large-scale ritual architecture – a temple, in effect – founded perhaps as early as 3500 BC, and used for two centuries or more. While details remain obscure, it seems that the next century or so saw further expansion of the southern state northwards and the earliest manifestations of the hieroglyphic script. Finally, around 3000 BC, the north of the country was absorbed, creating the state we know as Egypt.

Kingdoms, Periods and Dynasties

Egyptian history is divided into a series of 'Kingdoms' and 'Periods', and then sub-divided into 'Dynasties'. The latter are based upon a scheme drawn up by an Egyptian priest, Manetho, around 300 BC. He divided Egypt's kings into a series of numbered dynasties, corresponding to Europe's idea of royal 'houses' (e.g. Plantagenet, Habsburg, etc.). These broadly fit in with known changes in the ruling family, but in some cases the reason for a shift is unclear.

Ancient dating was by means of regnal years – that is, years within each monarch's reign – rather than the kind of 'era' dating used today (e.g. BC/AD or AH). Thus absolute dates, in terms of years BC, have to be established through various indirect methods. Some reigns can be fixed by links to events in better-dated cultures, while others can be placed by reference to mentions of various astronomical phenomena. Dates of other reigns can then be calculated from these fixed points. Nevertheless, there remain many areas of uncertainty and, while dating is solid back to 663 BC, margins of error before then may run in excess of a century.

Broadly speaking, the 'Kingdoms' denote eras of unity and power, the 'Periods', ones of disunity and/or foreign domination. The Archaic Period (First and Second Dynasties) is a formative time, which saw the consolidation of technology and literacy, but also civil war; this conflict may, however, ultimately have led to the establishment of the absolute royal power that underpinned the Old Kingdom (Third to Sixth Dynasties, c. 2700–2195 BC).

Land of the Pharaohs

It was the Old Kingdom that saw the building of the first – and greatest – pyramids, as well as many other architectural and artistic masterpieces; foreign trade flourished, too. The following First Intermediate Period witnessed a splintering of power, possibly the result of a failure of the Nile flood and consequent famine and disorder. At length, civil war brought unity under the Eleventh Dynasty, the first of the three houses that comprise the Middle Kingdom (c. 2000–1650 BC).

The dynasties of the Middle Kingdom recommenced major public works and trade, but royal power once again decayed under the Thirteenth Dynasty. Palestinian rulers appeared in the north-east delta, and eventually obtained control of the north of Egypt and, briefly, of the whole country. Ultimately, however, the Palestinians were driven out by the kings of Thebes (the main centre in the south), who then founded the Eighteenth Dynasty and the New Kingdom (c. 1550–1100 BC).

The New Kingdom was Egypt's imperial age, during which it obtained overlordship over much of Syria, Palestine and the northern part of Sudan. A brief official experiment with monotheism under Akhenaten was rapidly ended under his successor Tutankhamun; then, during the Nineteenth Dynasty, wealth and power began gradually to seep away. By the end of the Twentieth Dynasty, economic problems and civil strife had set in, and the succeeding Third Intermediate Period (21st to 25th Dynasties) saw a split in the country just south of the Fayoum. The senior king ruled from Tanis in the delta, while the south was ruled by a series of soldier-priests based on Thebes, some of whom were proclaimed pharaohs in their own right. Reunification came under the Sudanese Twnety-fifth Dynasty, but was followed by Assyrian invasion, and it was nearly a century more before central power was definitively re-established in the form of the Twenty-sixth Dynasty (also known as the Saite Period, 664–525 BC).

The Late Period (525–332 BC) was dominated by a struggle for independence from the Persian Empire. Three native dynasties in turn wrested control, but all were finally defeated by the Persians – who were then themselves overthrown by Alexander the Great. With the dissolution of Alexander's empire, Egypt came under the rule of the Macedonian Ptolemaic Dynasty for some three centuries, until the defeat of Kleopatra VII in 30 BC brought the country into the Roman Empire.

Above: A pharaoh in characteristic pose on the Seventh Pylon of the Greater Temple of Amun at Karnak: Thutmose III of the Eighteenth Dynasty smites his enemies.

The end of the Royal Pyramids

After royalty had abandoned pyramid burials at the beginning of the New Kingdom, the form came to be used by lesser members of society. These later monuments are outside the scope of this book, which attempts to provide a comprehensive listing of all pyramids built for the burial of a king or queen of Egypt.

EGYPTIAN TOMBS AND THE AFTERLIFE

Below: The Pyramid Texts – the earliest set of Egyptian texts dealing with the afterlife – first appear at the end of the Fifth Dynasty; this extract is from the pyramid of Teti (see pages 74–5).

The continued existence of the body on earth formed a key part of the ancient Egyptian view of the afterlife – visualized as a bigger and better Egypt. Consequently, provision of eternal accommodation for the body was granted high priority. For much of Egyptian history, the realm of the dead was envisaged as being ruled by the god Osiris, once an earthly divine king who was killed unjustly and then resurrected, as the first mummy, to rule the world of the dead.

The earliest set of texts dealing with the next world are the Pyramid Texts, inscribed inside the royal tombs of the late Fifth and Sixth Dynasties, although on internal evidence apparently composed generations before then. They deal specifically with the posthumous destiny of the king, which differed greatly from that of the mass of humanity: as a divine being he would dwell with his fellow gods in the entourage of the sun-god, Re. These texts are a miscellaneous compilation of spells of various kinds and lengths, with no two pyramids having precisely the same sets of spells; indeed, some are unique to a single tomb. They include instructions for ceremonies, hymns and spells to aid the progress and transformation of the spirit, possibly arranged in sets radiating out from the kernel of the pyramid, the sarcophagus.

Spirits of the dead

The spiritual part of the dead person was believed to have a number of aspects, including the *ka*, the *ba*, the *akh* and the 'shadow'. The *ba* was depicted as a human-headed bird, which was the

Right: Anubis, god of embalming; from the Nineteenth Dynasty temple of Sethy I at Abydos.

Below: The Giza necropolis, showing the mixture of rock-cut tombs and mastabas south-east of Khaefre's Pyramid. In the foreground is the tomb of Queen Khentkaues I (see page 123).

form in which the spirit travelled within and beyond the vicinity of the tomb. it would fly around or sit before the grave, taking its repose in the 'cool sweet breeze'. The concept of the *akh* was somewhat more esoteric, being the aspect of the dead in which he or she had ceased to be dead, having been transfigured into a living being. Viewed as a light in contrast to the darkness of death, the akh was often associated with the stars. The notion of the *ka* was even more complex, being an aspect of the person created at the same time as the body and surviving as its companion. It was the part of the deceased that was the immediate recipient of offerings, but had other functions, some of which remain obscure. However, whatever ethereal form the deceased took, it required sustenance for eternity, and it was from this fact that the fundamental facets of the tomb derived.

The Egyptian tomb comprised a number of basic components that are generally present in all of the myriad types of sepulchre known. Their appearance may vary considerably, but without an understanding of how each fits into the underlying scheme it is impossible to relate one monument to another.

Above: The kernel of the Egyptian tomb: the burial chamber. This chamber belongs to the Fourth Dynasty sepulchre of the courtier Debhen (LG90) at Giza, part of the rock-cut cemetery near the pyramid of Khaefre (see previous page).

Elements of the tomb

At its most fundamental level, a tomb is divided into two, and frequently three. At the core is the burial place itself (the substructure), containing the body. The physical corpse seems to have been the dead person's link with earth, the conduit of the sustenance received from the world of the living. It thus had to be kept incorrupt, and so the practice of mummification came into being: a technique of preserving the body by drying it out and wrapping it in bandages. Protection – both physical and magical – was ideally provided by one or more decorated coffins and, perhaps, a sarcophagus. To ensure security, the entrance to the burial chamber was blocked, and the approach shaft, corridor or stairway filled in. Safety might be further enhanced by the addition of plug-blocks or portcullis-slabs of hard stones, or by other architectural innovations which might make penetration by the omnipresent tomb-robber more difficult. Of course, this ideal state of protection for the dead was reached by the rich few only: most substructures were no more than holes in the desert.

The next element is the offering place, acting as the interface between this world and the hereafter in which the deceased dwelled. This was where offerings would be left by relatives and priests, or be generated by inscriptions and painted or carved tableaux. The latter concept was based on the Egyptian view that the writing or depiction of a thing could make it exist by means of magic – hence, many offering places featured images of food production to ensure that the dead person would go on being fed long after the last priest or relative had visited.

Offering places varied greatly in size and form. At the lowliest level, it would simply have been the place on the east side of the grave where a jar of beer and a loaf of bread might be left on feast days. At the other extreme, huge, elaborate temples with dozens of rooms would provide for the cult of the deceased. In between were many smaller chapels, which might be cut out of a cliff-face, erected against or within a built superstructure, or simply free-standing on the desert surface.

Many tombs added a third element: the superstructure. This could take a number of forms, the most characteristic being the mastaba – a low, bench-shaped building (the Arabic word 'mastaba' means 'bench') – and the pyramid. Both the mastaba and the pyramid can be solid, although mastabas often had chapels built within them, and the burial apartments of some pyramids penetrate into them. There are many tombs where the offering place and superstructure are so intimately entangled that it is not easy to analyze them separately.

These two or three elements could share the same site, being fully integrated with one another, or they could be separated, sometimes by distances of several miles. For example, during the New Kingdom, the substructure of a king's tomb was a set of corridors and chambers cut in the rock of a desert valley – the place known today as the Valley of the Kings – while the offering place was one of a

row of free-standing temples on the other side of a mountain, on the very edge of the desert and looking over the fields. The 'superstructure' was perhaps felt to be the mountain peak that overlooked the whole necropolis.

The offering place, or probably the courtyard in front of it, was the setting for the elaborate ceremonies that accompanied the funeral. Prior to this, the body would have been prepared by the embalmers. At its most perfect, attained during the New Kingdom, the process involved the removal from the body of all the internal organs – except the heart and kidneys – and its desiccation using a dry powder known as 'natron'. This is a mixture of salts, in particular sodium chloride – common salt – plus sodium bicarbonate, sodium carbonate and sodium sulphate, which was piled upon a stone slab; the corpse was laid on the salts, and then covered with a further layer of natron. After a number of weeks, the body was extracted and wrapped in bandages, as were the also-dessicated internal organs. The body was then placed in the coffin and the organs in the so-called 'canopic' containers: four jars and/or a chest. The details of the coffin (or nest of coffins) and the canopic containers varied over time: the former was rectangular until the Second Intermediate Period (c. 1650 BC), when mummy-shaped coffins began to replace the old design. Depending on the period and the status of the deceased, the coffin(s), of whatever shape, might be placed in a rectangular sarcophagus of stone or wood; the canopic chest generally matched the style of the sarcophagus.

Above: The offering place varied in size and form, but ideally contained depictions of the creation of food offerings and the deceased carrying out his or her daily life. This one belonged to the mayor Khnumhotep III of the Twelfth Dynasty, at Beni Hasan (BH3).

Mummification

In the Old Kingdom, mummification had taken a rather different form. Although natron seems to have been coming into use, the main aspect of the process was the

'We took our copper tools and forced a way into the pyramid of this king through its innermost part. We found the substructure, and we took our lighted candles in our hands and went down. Then we broke through the blocking that we found at the entrance to his crypt, and found this god lying at the back of his burial place.'

EXTRACT FROM THE CONFESSION OF THE ROBBERS OF THE PYRAMID OF SOBKEMSAF I, C. 1100 BC

tight wrapping of the individual limbs with linen, and then the application of a layer of plaster in which the individual's features were modelled. This contrasts with later mummies, where the limbs were lost from view amid the swathes of bandages and an all-enveloping outer shroud.

Throughout Egyptian history, the prepared mummy would be taken in procession to the tomb with the items to be placed with it in the burial chamber. The cortège would be accompanied by the mourning family and friends of the deceased, priests, and perhaps a host of professional mourners. The ceremonies of interment culminated in the ceremony of 'opening the mouth', in which the dead body was reanimated, involving implements that recalled those used at birth, including that which cut the umbilical cord.

The pyramids' enemies

Below: Napoleon Bonaparte's scientific team measuring the Great Sphinx in Giza in 1798.

After the completion of the ceremonies, the burial chamber was sealed and the spirit of the deceased set out on its journey to eternity. As envisioned in the New Kingdom and later (from 1550 BC), this involved overcoming the obstacles placed in its way by the guardians of the various gates that lay between it and its goal, the 'Hall of Judgment'. Here, Osiris, King of the Dead, presided over the weighing of the deceased's heart — regarded as the seat of intelligence and knowledge — against the feather of *maat*, the personification of truth, order and justice. If the pans of the scale balanced, the dead person would come before Osiris and pass into life eternal. If the heart proved heavier, it would be fed to a monster named 'the Devourer', and the spirit cast into the darkness. However,

the magical 'guidebooks' supplied for the deceased – the best known being the 'Book of the Dead', introduced in the New Kingdom – contained spells guaranteeing the spirit success in its great journey.

Although magic could guarantee that the spirit's journey to 'the West' was as effortless as possible, the main threat to its well-being was on earth: the tomb-robber. From the earliest times, tempted by the rich grave-goods placed in high-status tombs, robbers would penetrate sepulchres and strip them of their contents. Indeed, tombs have been found still sealed, but wrecked: evidence that those charged with the burial had ransacked the body and its equipment, probably before the mourners had even got back home. In spite of harsh penalties – the preferred penalty for tomb-robbers seems to have been impalement – at certain periods tomb-robbery became endemic. Records survive of the trials of those accused of robbing royal tombs in the time of Rameses IX (*c.* 1100 BC), including the pyramid of Sobkemsaf I.

Following the final collapse of the

Above: Jacques de Morgan holds aloft the circlet of Princess Khnemet, having just removed it from her mummy in the funerary complex of her father, Amenemhat II, at Dahshur.

ancient Egyptian civilization and religion in the face of the forces of Christianity and Islam, the old cities of the dead lost their last remaining shreds of sanctity and physical protection, and many tombs fell victim to the monotheistic iconoclasts and treasure-seekers. Medieval Arabic accounts tell, often with wondrous embellishments, of ventures into the pyramids and tombs to recover their riches. However, by the 16th century AD, the first real signs of European interest in ancient Egypt were becoming apparent, beginning the process that would culminate in the scientific resurrection of its monuments from the 19th century.

The first manifestation of this enthusiasm for reclamation was a horrifying free-for-all in the early 19th century, in which monuments were disfigured or even destroyed to garner objects for Western museums and private collections. Matters improved with the foundation of the national Egyptian Antiquities Service in 1858 and the consequent licensing of excavations. Today, all fieldwork in Egypt is tightly regulated; all discoveries are recorded, and very few objects are allowed to leave the country. Vast amounts of new information are published every year, with fresh data leading to frequent revisions of the interpretation of even long-known monuments.

THE EGYPTIAN PYRAMID COMPLEX

It is important to recognize that in spite of their monumental size, the royal pyramids of the Old and Middle Kingdoms conform precisely to the 'generic' tomb structure described in the previous chapter. They do, however, add further elements to produce what is known as the 'Pyramid Complex'. While there are of course deviations from the norm – particularly during the earliest and latest phases of pyramid building – the basic components are constant.

The Substructure

Usually, the burial chamber lies below the approximate centre of the superstructure, oriented east–west, with a stone sarcophagus at the western end. A square stone chest – the canopic chest for the embalmed internal organs – is frequently sunk in the paving to the south-east. Outside the burial chamber may be an antechamber and perhaps a store-room, from which a passage leads towards the exterior. Until the middle of the Twelfth Dynasty, the entrance was placed in the middle of the north face of the pyramid. The entrance passageway was normally interrupted by up to three portcullis slabs of granite, lowered to block the corridor after the funeral. The sloping outer part of the entrance – the descending passage – was generally filled with rubble, or large plug-blocks of stone, slid in from the outside. The actual entrance lay either on the face of the pyramid or just in front of it. In both cases the entrance was sealed with stone blocks – supposedly for eternity.

The substructure was usually built in a cutting in the bedrock, which was then concealed under the pyramid. A few examples exist of the substructure being tunnelled out of rock, but the 'cut and cover' approach was far more common. It had the great advantage of allowing heavy items like sarcophagi and portcullis slabs to be installed by being lowered in from above, rather than manhandled through the low and narrow passages of the substructure.

Below: The key to the whole purpose of the pyramid was the burial chamber. In most cases this had a pointed roof, and this typical construction is shown clearly in the ruined pyramid of Queen Neferhetepes at Saqqara (see page 124).

The Offering Place(s)

On the east side of the pyramid is the mortuary temple. The focus of this is against the face of the pyramid, where there is generally found a false door stela – a slab of stone carved as a stylized doorway, representing the physical interface between the earthly world and the next. Alternatively, or in addition, there may be an offering table to perform a similar role of taking offerings and passing them to the dead king.

The temples of the earliest pyramids had a pair of stelae flanking the offering table, but very little outside this enclosed sanctuary area. However, as time went by, additional elements were added. Typically, a room with five niches for statues lay just outside the sanctuary, as did various corridors and store-rooms. This inner complex was fronted by a courtyard, surrounded by a pillar-supported porch – the peristyle court. In front of the courtyard stood a solid walled entrance hall as the gateway to the temple, decorated, like much of the building, with scenes showing the king in the presence of the gods and offerings being brought for the benefit of his spirit.

In addition to the mortuary temple, a small chapel is often found in the middle of the north face, over or adjacent to the entrance of the pyramid. Like the mortuary temple, the chapel would have been built of limestone, with details and paving in harder stones, including columns of granite from Aswan, far up the Nile.

'May heaven rain with fresh myrrh, may it drip with incense upon the roof of the temple of King Seneferu.'

AKHEPERKARESONBE, c. 1475 BC

The Pyramid

Except in the earliest stages of its development, a royal pyramid of the Old and Middle Kingdoms is a straight-sided structure rising at an angle of around 52 degrees. Its size varies greatly with time; while the majority are around 80 metres square, the largest examples run up to well over 200 metres square. Heights range up to 146 metres, although around 50 metres is most common. The overall aspect was a dazzling white, derived from the fine-quality Tura limestone that was used for the outer layers of the monument. Tura limestone was taken from the eponymous quarries on the east bank of the Nile opposite many of the pyramid sites.

Left: Until the appearance of the Pyramid Texts, substructures were generally unadorned, with the exception of such items as the panelling found in this vestibule in the Third Pyramid at Giza (see pages 62–3).

The cores of most pyramids were built from lower-quality limestone quarried adjacent to the building site. The size of the blocks varied with time: the largest and best squared are found early in the pyramid sequence. Some of the later pyramids had cores of sun-dried mud brick, the principal building material of Ancient Egypt. All pyramids depended heavily on their Tura limestone casings for long-term stability. This stone was coveted by later builders, and nearly all pyramids were stripped of their casings during ancient and medieval times. The result is that many pyramids are now little better than mounds of rubble, with only the earlier, better-built examples retaining something of their original form.

The Subsidiary Pyramid

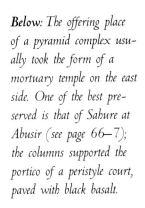

Below: The offering place of a pyramid complex usually took the form of a mortuary temple on the east side. One of the best preserved is that of Sahure at Abusir (see page 66–7); the columns supported the portico of a peristyle court, paved with black basalt.

A feature of all but the very latest pyramid complexes was a dummy tomb, usually in the form of a small, steeply angled pyramid. This initially lay opposite the centre of the south face of the main pyramid, but came ultimately to be placed south of the sanctuary of the mortuary temple.

The purpose of this dummy tomb is unknown, although many suggestions have been made. It can best be characterized as 'ritual' – archaeological shorthand for 'of unknown purpose, but clearly important'!

The Causeway and Valley Building

A royal pyramid could lie anywhere up to 1,500 metres west of the desert edge, east of which lay fields, canal networks and the Nile. This gap was bridged by a stone causeway that terminated in the entrance hall of the mortuary temple. The causeway was decorated in the same way as the temple, and generally had a roof. A surviving causeway (at Unas' pyramid) was lit by a slot down the centre of the ceiling.

Access to the causeway was via the valley building, so called as it was on the desert edge nearest the river. The valley building usually had one or more quays

where boats could dock, either on a canal or when the flood waters covered everything up to the desert edge. Centred on a pillared hall, the valley building also played a role in the royal cult; in at least one case it became the principal place where offerings were left after the mortuary temple itself fell out of use.

Other Elements

A king's pyramid complex was generally a focus for other high-status burials. In particular, the king's wives were interred nearby. Most had small pyramids, but others had mastabas or even rock-cut tombs. Although locations vary, it is common to find queens' tombs on the east side of the king's pyramid, particularly in the north-east quadrant.

The tombs of the nobility and lesser members of the royal family were initially kept well away from the king's tomb complex, but during the Fourth Dynasty this tendency was radically reversed, with huge cemeteries purposely built close to the Great Pyramid at Giza. This strictly planned approach did not last, but in future the standing of an individual could be measured by the proximity of his tomb to that of his king.

N

Sanctuary, with false-door stela

Five statue-niches

Enclosure wall

Subsidiary pyramid

Peristyle court

Store chambers

Entrance hall

Causeway to valley building

Above: Plan of a typical Fifth/Sixth Dynasty mortuary temple.

Left: The causeway ultimately evolved into a covered corridor leading from the edge of the desert to the mortuary temple. This causeway connects the elements of Unas' complex (see pages 72–3).

EXPLORING THE PYRAMIDS

The pyramids have always attracted attention. They were tourist destinations as early as the Eighteenth Dynasty, as we know from graffiti at Saqqara, Dahshur and Meidum. Early in the next dynasty, Prince Khaemwaset, High Priest of Ptah and son of Rameses II, was undertaking antiquarian investigations and carving the name of the pyramid's founder on the casings of a number of pyramids.

Below: The English traveller, George Sandys (1578–1644) approaches the pyramids of Giza in 1611.

The Twenty-fifth and Twenty-sixth dynasties saw a revival in ancient art styles, and a number of pyramids were entered. In Menkaure's pyramid, the king's broken body was provided with a new coffin, while a new entrance gallery was pushed under the Step Pyramid of Djoser. Here, copies were made of the reliefs in the underground chambers, as shown by the grids drawn over them in ink.

The ancient Greeks and Romans also flocked to the pyramid field. The fifth-century BC historian Herodotus records the tall tales told to him by his guides at Giza, which compare well with some of those told today. However, with the absorption of Egypt into the Islamic world in AD 640, Western travellers largely disappeared. Knowledge of the pyramids' true purpose had become hazy with the collapse of paganism in the fourth and fifth centuries, and they came frequently to be called the 'Granaries of Joseph', allegedly built by the patriarch in the years of plenty.

'Full West of the City, close upon those desarts, a-loft on a rocky level adjoyoning to the valley, stand those three Pyramides (the barbarous monuments of prodicgality and vain-glory) so universally celebrated.'

GEORGE SANDYS, 1610

Others, however, did realize that the pyramids were tombs, and thus also potential treasure-houses. Many pyramids show signs of mediaeval investigations, most famously the Great Pyramid of Giza. Contemporary writers recorded the Caliph Maamun cutting or enlarging a tunnel in the north face of the pyramid and penetrating the interior. What he found is not totally clear, but it seems to have included human remains. Whether or not these belonged to the pyramid's founder, Khufu, remains a moot point.

Other investigators were more interested in the pyramids as sources of raw materials. The fine limestone casings were stripped off almost all pyramids that still had them – many had gone in pharaonic times – and the same stone was also ripped from interiors, leaving many Fifth and Sixth dynasty pyramids in a sorry condition.

The Europeans

European travellers began to reappear in the 17th century AD, with the first 'scientific' survey at Giza being made by John Greaves in 1639–40. Useful work was done over the next century by a variety of individuals, but real advances came only with the French military campaign of 1798, which also included a large contingent of scholars. Their research sparked a resurgence of interest in Ancient Egypt and the creation of national collections of its antiquities. The resulting market was supplied in part by the various European consuls in Egypt who, on a purely freelance basis, collected material and also hired others to do so on their behalf. The British Consul Henry Salt (1780–1827) employed the Italian archaeologist Giovanni Belzoni, while later Colonel Patrick Campbell (1779–1857) sponsored Richard Vyse's work at Giza.

Nationally sponsored scientific expeditions were sent to Egypt by France and Prussia in 1828 and 1842–5, respectively; the latter, under Carl Lepsius, was responsible for the first comprehensive cataloguing and mapping of the pyramids. They were, however, little considered by the new Egyptian Antiquities Service, founded by the Viceroy in 1858, and whose first director was the French Egyptologist François Mariette. Apparently devoid of inscriptions, the pyramids were deemed unlikely to repay the effort needed to open the large number that remained unexplored.

Just how wrong this assumption was became apparent with the discovery of the Pyramid Texts by the German Brugsch brothers in 1881 – a breakthrough that was rapidly followed by the opening of a large number of pyramids by Maspero during the early 1880s. At the same time, William Petrie undertook an elaborate survey of the Giza plateau, beginning a career that included the excavation of a whole range of pyramids by him and his associates, based at University College London.

Among the pyramids investigated by Petrie were particular examples from the Middle Kingdom, knowledge of which was further enhanced in the 1890s by work undertaken by de Morgan, Gautier and Jéquier for the Antiquities Service. This pattern of work, conducted in parallel by both the Egyptian authorities and foreign teams, has continued to the present day.

A Plan of the Pyramids of Saccara, and Dashour.

Above: Richard Pococke's 1739 map of the pyramid fields of Saqqara and Dahshur.

Below: Gaston Maspero, successor to Mariette, seen here inside the pyramid of Unas. Maspero undertook the full study of the Pyramid Texts, and in the 1880s he opened most of those pyramids that had, until then, remained closed.

Above: John Perring, whose solo survey of the pyramid sites in 1838–39, and his work with Richard Howard Vyse at Giza in 1837, make him perhaps the greatest of all pyramid explorers.

Right: Excavations continue today; here, a Czech expedition to Abusir clears the ruined substructure of Neferefre in December 1997. The roofing of the chambers was removed centuries ago, but the bottom of the entrance corridor can be seen at the far end of the excavation.

Particular examples of Egyptian discoveries have been the pyramid complexes of Djoser, Isesi, Unas, Userkaf, Sekhemkhet, Pepy II, Khendjer and Seneferu (the Bent Pyramid), while foreign teams have contributed to the investigation of such sites as Giza, Saqqara-South, Dahshur, Mazghuna, Lisht, Meidum, Lahun and Hawara.

Recent activity

In recent years much work has been devoted to revisiting sites excavated in the past, to check data and search for what may have been missed. Perhaps the most important of all such investigations have been the surveys made by Maragioglio and Rinaldi in the 1960s and 1970s, which recorded in great detail everything that was then visible or could be accessed from earlier publications. Unfortunately, only seven of the projected 14 volumes of their report appeared prior to the researchers' deaths.

Others have undertaken new excavations and, today, years may be devoted to one pyramid. Back in 1894–95, de Morgan excavated three Dahshur monuments in an aggregate of only half a year's work; now, Arnold's seven and 12 (so far) years' work, respectively, in the pyramid complexes of Amenemhat III and Senwosret III at Dahshur has found not only new details, but whole new galleries and chambers! Painstaking work has allowed the shattered chamber walls of Pepy I and Nemtyemsaf I to be restored, while even the intensively dug site of Giza still springs surprises. In 1991, Hawass discovered the remains of Khufu's subsidiary pyramid, and he also continued with the excavation of the village occupied by the men who built the pyramids there. The exploration of the pyramids is by no means over.

Pyramid Explorers

Giovanni Belzoni: pioneer excavator and the first European to enter the Second Pyramid at Giza.

ALY, Mohammed A.
Egyptian archaeologist; Inspector of Antiquities at Edfu in 1980.

AMÉLINEAU, Émile
(1850–1915) French Egyptologist. Professor of History of Religions at the École des Hautes Études, Paris. Excavated at Abydos, 1894–8.

ARNOLD, Dieter
German Egyptologist. Excavated for German Archaeological Institute, Cairo, and now a Curator in the Metropolitan Museum of Art, New York.

AYRTON, Edward Russell
(1882–1914) English archaeologist. Excavated for the Egypt Exploration Fund 1902–1905, and then in the Valley of the Kings. He subsequently worked in Ceylon, where he drowned while hunting.

BALLERINI, Francesco
(1877–1910) Italian Egyptologist, on the staff of the Egyptian Museum, Turin.

BARSANTI, Alessandro
(1858–1917) Italian archaeologist and conservator. Worked for the Egyptian Antiquities Service throughout Egypt.

BÁRTA, Miroslav
Czech Egyptologist.

BELZONI, Giovanni Battista
(1778–1823) Italian archaeologist and explorer. Employed by the British Consul to collect antiquities, 1816–18, and made a number of major discoveries. Died of dysentery while exploring in West Africa.

BORCHARDT, Ludwig
(1863–1938) German Egyptologist. Director of German Archaeological Institute in Cairo; excavated at Abusir and Amarna.

BRUGSCH, Émile
(1842–1930) German Egyptologist. Assistant Conservator of Egyptian Museum, 1870–1914. First European to enter a pyramid containing Pyramid Texts, and also discovered the cache of royal mummies at Deir el-Bahari, all in 1880–81.

BRUGSCH, Heinrich Ferdinand Karl
(1827–1894) German Egyptologist and brother of Émile. Professor of Egyptology at Göttingen; worked on the Pyramid Texts.

BRUNTON, Guy
(1878–1948) English Egyptologist. Assistant Keeper of Cairo Museum 1931–48. Previously had excavated widely in Egypt.

CAILLIAUD, Frédéric
(1787–1869) French mineralogist. Travelled extensively in Egypt and Nubia both professionally and on his own account, 1815–22.

CAPART, Jean
(1877–1947) Belgian Egyptologist. Professor of Egyptology at University of Liège.

CARTER, Howard
(1874–1939) English archaeologist and artist. Chief Inspector for Upper Egypt 1899–1904; later excavated for the Earl of Carnarvon, discovering the tomb of Tutankhamun in 1922.

CAVIGLIA, Giovanni Battista
(1770–1845) Genoese mariner. Excavated at Giza, 1816–36, ultimately for Vyse.

CHASSINAT, Émile Gaston
(1868–1948) French Egyptologist. Director of French Institute for Oriental Archaeology, Cairo, 1898–1911; worked at a number of sites in Egypt and published many religious texts from major temples.

CURRELLY, Charles Trick
(1876–1957) Canadian Egyptologist. Excavated with the Egypt Exploration Fund from 1902; Director of the Royal Ontario Museum, Toronto, 1914–46.

DARESSY, Georges Émile Jules
(1864–1938) French Egyptologist. Assistant Keeper of Cairo Museum 1887–1923.

DAVISON, Nathaniel
(d. 1809) British diplomat. Travelled in the Levant from 1763 and excavated and explored in Egypt; Consul-General at Algiers 1780–83.

DE MAILLET, Benoît
(1656–1738) French Consul-General in Egypt 1692–1708.

DE MORGAN, Jacques Jean Marie
(1857–1924) French archaeologist. Director of the Egyptian Antiquities Service 1892–7; excavated at Susa in Iran.

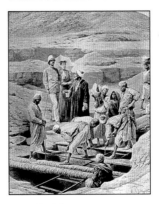

Jacques De Morgan supervises excavations in the pyramid complex of Senwosret III; the shaft leads to the tombs of the king's family.

DREYER, Günter
German Egyptologist. Director of the German Archaeological Institute, Cairo.

DUFFERIN and AVA, Frederick Temple Hamilton-Temple Blackwood, Marquess of
(1826–1902) Irish statesman. Travelled in Egypt 1858–9.

EL-KHOULI, Ali
Egyptian Egyptologist.

EL-MALLAKH, Kamal
Egyptian architect and archaeologist.

ENGELBACH, Reginald (Rex)
(1888–1946) English Egyptologist. Worked with Petrie from 1910 and then as Chief Inspector for Upper Egypt 1920; Assistant and then Chief Keeper of Cairo Museum 1924–41.

Rex Engelbach worked with Petrie for a number of years and was responsible for exploring the pyramids of Mazghuna.

FARAG, Naguib
Egyptian archaeologist. Inspector of Antiquities at Medinet el-Fayoum in the mid-1950s.

FAKHRY, Ahmed
(1905–1973) Egyptian archaeologist; held various Inspectorates of Antiquities from 1932 onwards until he became Professor of Ancient History at Cairo in 1952.

FIRTH, Cecil Mallaby
(1878–1931) English archaeologist. Inspector of Antiquities at Saqqara from 1923.

FISHER, Clarence Stanley
(1876–1941) American archaeologist. Excavated widely in the Near East.

GABRA, Sami
(1892–1979) Egyptian Egyptologist. Professor of Ancient History, Cairo University, 1930–52; best known for excavations at Tuna el-Gebel.

GAUTIER, Joseph Étienne
(1861–1924) French archaeologist. Excavated widely in Egypt and the Middle East.

GONEIM, Mohammed Zakaria
(1911–59) Egyptian archaeologist. Inspector, then Keeper, of the Theban Necropolis 1939–51; Keeper of Saqqara from 1951. Found dead in Nile in 1959.

GREAVES, John
(1602–52) English mathematician and astronomer. Professor of Astronomy at Oxford 1640–48.

HABACHI, Labib
(1906–84) Egyptian Egyptologist. Chief Inspector of a number of areas 1944–58; wrote extensively on historical and archaeological matters.

HARVEY, Stephen P.
American Egyptologist. Assistant Professor of Egyptian Art and Archaeology, University of Chicago.

HASSAN, Selim
(1886–1961) Egyptian Egyptologist. Professor of Egyptology, Cairo University, from 1931.

HAWASS, Zahi
Egyptian Egyptologist. For many years in charge of the Memphite necropolis, and head of the Supreme Council for Antiquities from 2002.

HÖLSCHER, Uvo
(1878–1963) German archaeologist. Professor at the Technical High School in Hanover.

HUSSEIN, Abdelsalam Mohammed
(d. 1949) Egyptian archaeologist. Director of the Pyramids Study Project from 1945 until the end of his life. He worked successively on the pyramid of Isesi, the Red Pyramid and the Bent Pyramid until his death in the USA. Unfortunately his excavation notes have never been located.

ISKANDER, Zaki
(1916–79) Egyptian conservator. Principal scientist of the Antiquities Service for many years, finishing his career as Director General of Egyptian Antiquities Organization, and holding a number of university chairs.

JÉQUIER, Gustave
(1868–1946) Swiss Egyptologist. Excavated widely for the Institut Français d'Archéologie Orientale and the Egyptian Antiquities Service.

KAMAL, Ahmed
(1849–1923) The first Egyptian Egyptologist. Assistant Curator of the Cairo Museum; dug widely in Egypt.

LABROUSSE, Audran
French archaeologist. Director of the French Archaeological Mission of Saqqara.

LACAU, Pierre Lucien
(1873–1963) French Egyptologist. Director of the Antiquities Service 1914–36, and Professor of Egyptology at the Collège de France from 1938.

LANSING, Ambrose
(1891–1959) American Egyptologist. Curator of Egyptian Department of Metropolitan Museum of Art, New York.

LAUER, Jean-Philippe
(1902–2001) French architect

and archaeologist. Excavated at Saqqara from 1926 onwards.

LECLANT, Jean
French Egyptologist. Professor of Egyptology at the Collège de France, Paris.

LEPSIUS, Carl Richard
(1810–84) German Egyptologist. Keeper of the Egyptian Museum, Berlin.

Carl Lepsius, leader of the great Prussian expedition of the 1840s and inveterate cataloguer of pyramids. His numbering system remains in use today.

LORET, Victor Clément Georges Philippe
(1859–1946) French Egyptologist. Director of Egyptian Antiquities Service 1897–9.

LYTHGOE, Albert Morton
(1868–1934) American Egyptologist. Curator of Egyptian Art at Metropolitan Museum of Art, New York.

MACE, Arthur Cruttenden
(1874–1928) English archaeologist. Associate Curator of Egyptian Art at Metropolitan Museum of Art, New York.

MACKAY, Ernest John Henry
(1880–1943) English archaeologist. Worked with Petrie from 1907, and then in Mesopotamia and India from 1919.

MAKRAMALLAH, Rizkallah
(1903–49) Egyptian archaeologist. Assistant Director of Works at Saqqara 1931–7; Chief Inspector for Upper

Egypt 1937–9, later Lecturer at Cairo and Alexandria Universities.

MARAGIOGLIO, Vita Giuseppe
(1915–76) Italian army officer and archaeologist. Undertook extensive survey of pyramid sites with Rinaldi from the 1950s onwards.

MARIETTE, François Auguste Ferdinand
(1821–81) French Egyptologist. Employed at Louvre from 1849; in 1858 founded Egyptian Antiquities Service, of which he remained Director until his death.

Auguste Mariette, founder of the Egyptian Antiquities Service. He undertook relatively little work on pyramids, believing them to be 'mute', or devoid of inscriptions. It was only on his deathbed that he learned of the existence of the Pyramid Texts.

MASPERO, Gaston Camille Charles
(1846–1916) French Egyptologist. Director of Egyptian Antiquities Service 1881–6 and 1899–1914.

MATHIEU, Bernard
French Egyptologist. Director of Institut Français d'Archéologie Orientale.

MELTON, Edward
(c. 1635–after 1677) English traveller; travelled extensively in the Levant and West Indies between 1660 and 1677.

MILLET, Nicholas
American Egyptologist. Curator responsible for the Egyptian collections at the

Royal Ontario Museum, Toronto.

MINUTOLI, Johann Heinrich Benjamin Menu, Freiherr von
(1772–1846) Prussian soldier. Travelled in Egypt 1820–21.

MOND, Sir Robert
(1867–1938) British chemist and excavator. Sponsored numerous excavations; President of Egypt Exploration Society from 1929.

MOUSSA, Ahmed
Egyptian archaeologist. Chief Inspector at Saqqara.

MUSES, Charles Arthur
(1919–2000) American mathematician and scientist. Excavated at Heliopolis and Dahshur in 1957.

NAVILLE, Henri Édouard
(1844–1926) Swiss Egyptologist. Professor of Egyptology at the University of Geneva; excavated widely for Egypt Exploration Fund.

PALANQUE, Charles
(1865–1910) French Egyptologist. Excavated at a number of sites for the Institut Français d'Archéologie Orientale.

PERRING, John Shae
(1813–69) English civil engineer. Worked in Egypt 1836–40.

PETRIE, Sir William Matthew Flinders
(1853–1942) English Egyptologist. Professor of Egyptology at University College London 1892–1933.

POCOCKE, Richard
(1704–65) English clergyman. Travelled in Near East 1737–40.

POLZ, Daniel
German Egyptologist. Deputy Director of German Institute from 1998.

QUIBELL, James Edward
(1867–1935) English archaeologist. Chief Inspector of

Flinders Petrie began his long career surveying at Giza in 1880. Here, he is outside the rock-cut tomb-chapel that he (and previous visitors) used for lodgings.

Antiquities 1898–1913, and then Keeper of Cairo Museum until 1923.

REISNER, George Andrew
(1867–1942) American Egyptologist. Curator of the Egyptian Department, Museum of Fine Arts, Boston.

RIFAUD, Jean Jacques
(1786–1852) French excavator. Worked on behalf of the French Consul, Bernardino Drovetti, 1816–26.

RINALDI, Celeste
(1902–77) Italian civil engineer. Undertook extensive survey of pyramid sites with Maragioglio from the 1950s onwards.

ROWE, Alan
(1891–1968) English archaeologist. Excavated for Pennsylvania University Museum and Harvard–Boston expedition to Giza; Curator of Graeco-Roman Museum, Alexandria, 1940–49, and subsequently taught at Manchester University.

SAAD, Zaki Youssef
(1901–82) Egyptian Egyptologist. Excavated at various sites in Lower Egypt; Director of Inspectorates of the Antiquities Service 1954–60.

SAINTE FARE GARNOT, Jean (1908–63) French Egyptologist. Director of

Institut Français d'Archéologie Orientale, 1953–59, and then Professor of Egyptology at the Sorbonne, Paris.

SANDYS, George
(1578–1644) English traveller. Made extensive foreign tour from 1610.

SCHIAPARELLI, Ernesto
(1856–1928) Italian Egyptologist. Director of the Egyptian Museum, Turin, 1894–1927.

SEGATO, Girolamo
(1792–1836) Italian explorer. Excavated and explored in Egypt, 1818–22.

SHAHIN, Mohammed
(*fl.* 1880) Chief Workman for Egyptian Antiquities Service.

STADELMANN, Rainer
(b. 1933) German Egyptologist; joined German Archaeological Institute, Cairo, in 1968; Director 1989–98.

SWELIM, Nabil M. A.
Egyptian Egyptologist and naval officer; retired as Commodore. Received his PhD. from Eötvös Loránd University, Budapest in 1982.

VALLOGGIA, Michel
Swiss Egyptologist.

VARILLE, Alexandre
(1909–51) French Egyptologist. Excavated for Institut Français

d'Archéologie Orientale and Egyptian Antiquities Service.

VERNER, Miroslav
Czech Egyptologist. Professor of Egyptology at Charles University, Prague.

VYSE, Richard William Howard
(1784–1853) English army officer. Excavated in Egypt 1835–7.

WAINWRIGHT, Gerald Avery
(1879–1964) English archaeologist. Excavated for Petrie and the Egypt Exploration Society; Chief Inspector for the Antiquities Service in Middle Egypt 1921–24.

WEIGALL, Arthur Edward Pearse Brome
(1880–1934) English Egyptologist. Excavated with Petrie from 1901; Inspector-General of Antiquities for Upper Egypt 1905–14. Subsequently author, journalist and theatre designer.

WEILL, Raymond
(1874–1950) French Egyptologist. Excavated at various sites in Egypt.

WILBOUR, Charles Edwin
(1833–96) American traveller and copyist. Spent the last two decades of his life travelling in Egypt.

WILKINSON, (Sir) John Gardner Wilkinson
(1797–1875) English Egyptologist. Lived in Egypt 1821–33 and visited in 1843 and 1848–9, studying and copying the monuments.

WINLOCK, Herbert Eustis
(1884–1950) American Egyptologist. Excavated for Metropolitan Museum of Art from 1906 until 1931, when he became the museum's Director.

WOOD, Robert
(*c.* 1717–71) British traveller. Travelled in Egypt in 1843 and 1750–51.

VISITING THE PYRAMIDS

With the exceptions of Seneferu's miniature pyramids, which are spread along the length of Egypt, all the royal pyramids lie within reach of a day trip from Egypt's capital, Cairo. Almost all are situated close to the north–south Agricultural Road, and to the main route to Upper Egypt, which runs closer to the west bank of the Nile. Anyone intending to make more than one excursion to pyramid sites during their stay in Cairo would be well advised to stay in a hotel in Giza, the portion of Greater Cairo on the west of the river.

Below: Visitors descend from the Red Pyramid at Dahshur after the arduous but rewarding trip to the spectacular corbelled chambers inside.

Although the new ring road has greatly improved matters, it can still be a long haul through traffic-clogged streets from the centre of Cairo to the west. This said, there is far more to do and see 'downtown' than out in Giza, so the visitor must prioritize!

Many tour companies run trips to pyramid sites. The most common formula is to visit Giza and Saqqara, often as a single day's outing, though some simply do Giza, paired with the Egyptian Museum. Specialist operators, on the other hand, target enthusiasts and run week-long excursions that aim to cover as many monuments as humanly possible. It is perfectly feasible to 'do' most sites as an independent traveller, generally by hiring a taxi for the day: car hire is not recommended, given the nature of Egyptian traffic. For the budget traveller, there is plenty of local transport, although this will require plenty of planning – and probably plenty of walking as well!

It must be noted that access to sites and monuments changes regularly in accordance with the demands of restoration, staffing and other issues. It is, therefore, important to check the latest situation before setting off on a long trip. Access usually requires the purchase of a ticket, as does interior – and occasionally exterior – photography. Tipping of *gaffirs* (guardians) is optional, but any particular act of kindness certainly deserves recognition.

Above: Two intact boat-pits have been found along the south side of the Great Pyramid at Giza. The huge cedar boat from one of the pits has been reassembled in the Solar Boat Museum above, which has been built directly over the pit. The other boat remains sealed in its pit, awaiting further investigations.

Giza and beyond

The most straightforward visit is to the Giza pyramids that lie at the end of Sharia Ahram (Pyramids Street), where modern houses, shops, offices and hotels extend right to the edge of the desert. They are within walking distance or a short taxi ride of local hotels, and can be reached from elsewhere in the city by air-conditioned bus, ordinary bus or taxi. The authorities are trying to cut back on vehicles on the plateau itself, so the visitor needs to be prepared to walk the last hundred metres or so – which is in any case the best way to approach the site. There is an entry ticket for the plateau as a whole, but you will also need separate tickets for some of the individual monuments. Tickets for the Great Pyramid, for example, are strictly limited in number each day to reduce the damage caused by visitors.

The mountain of Abu Rowash, with Djedefre's pyramid on top, can be seen clearly from Giza, and also from the elevated ring road. As of 2002, it is not routinely open to visitors, although, as with all 'closed' sites, permission to visit can be obtained from the site director's office near the Great

Above: The central atrium of the Cairo Museum houses the largest objects of the museum's collection, among which are the cap-stones of the pyramids of Amenhemhat III and Khendjer, both in the centre foreground.

Pyramid. The most straightforward access is from the Cairo–Alexandria Desert Road, from which a track leads towards the pyramid. The Brick Pyramid lies within the area of Abu Rowash village, close to the Agricultural Road and the area in which local children now play soccer.

Zawiyet el-Aryan is largely taken up by a military base, which completely encloses the Unfinished Pyramid and whose perimeter wall runs close to the Layer Pyramid. Access to the Unfinished Pyramid is impossible, and the latter should not be approached without the company of an Antiquities Inspector.

Abusir is not officially open and for the time being can only be visited 'unofficially'. The site can be reached either via a right turn alongside a canal on the road from Memphis to Saqqara (see below), or from the north, by a road that branches off the main road a little south of Giza. This 'scenic' route allows a clear, distant, view of the Layer Pyramid.

Saqqara and beyond

Saqqara, reached via the villages of Bedashrein and Mit Rahina (the site of ancient Memphis), is well organized for the visitor. The site entrance ticket covers most of the monuments. Of the pyramids of Saqqara, only one interior is normally accessible – either that of Teti or that of Unas. Additionally, the enclosure of the Step Pyramid may be visited, but not its interior.

The pyramids of Saqqara-South are not formally 'open', and are difficult to reach without four-wheel-drive transport. An ordinary car could reach the foot of Isesi's causeway, from where it is a long desert walk to the other monuments. The largely vanished Thirteenth Dynasty pyramids are cut off from the site by a railway line.

Access to Dahsur is via the main north–south road, with a right turn through the village of Minshat Dahshur. A paved road leads to the Red Pyramid, whose interior is open and lit, while a dirt road leads on to the Bent Pyramid, which may be opened in due course. The Middle Kingdom pyramids along the front of the necropolis are more problematic. It is possible to follow the line of the Bent Pyramid's causeway down to its valley building, from where a stiff walk brings one to the Black Pyramid – this can also be reached via a track alongside the canal outside the entrance to the site proper. The almost vanished White Pyramid requires a scramble up a steep bank of soft sand. The pyramid of Senwosret III lies beyond the gas works to the right of the site entrance but at the time of writing was under excavation.

The pyramids of Dahshur-South and Mazghuna are very difficult to reach. Moreover, they are in such a state of ruin that they are almost impossible to locate! In contrast, the Lisht monuments are easily visible from the road; the usual means of access is through the village at the south end of the site, which brings one out at the modern cemetery behind Senwosret I's pyramid. Neither this one, nor that of Amenemhat I, which requires a fairly long desert walk, can be entered, although many elements of the pyramid complexes can still be recognized.

Above: The dramatic shape of the pyramid of Meidum is visible from far away across the green fields that approach to within 100 metres of the base of the monument.

Hawara, Lahun and Meidum

Hawara, Lahun and Meidum lie on the margins of the Fayoum. The Hawara monument is visible from the main road: various fragments of stone sculpture and architectural elements lie around the area of the Labyrinth, and it is possible to enter the pyramid, albeit only for a short distance, after which point the corridor is filled with water. Continuing along the road beyond Amenemhat III's pyramid and crossing a bridge, one arrives at the ruined pyramid of Neferuptah, just to the right of the road. Lahun is difficult to get to; access is either via the narrow streets of the nearby village, or from the area of its valley building, with a bone-shaking ride up to the pyramid itself. It cannot be entered, but the tombs of the royal family are clearly visible.

As one approaches Meidum, there are many spectacular vistas from the main north–south highway. The interior and mortuary temple are both open, and it is also possible to view the interior of the large mastaba that lies adjacent to the pyramid. A large cluster of ruined mastabas lies some distance to the north. Of the small pyramids attributed to Seneferu, few are visitable without specialist knowledge and an escort from the Supreme Council of Antiquities. The principal exception is that at Zawiyet Sultan, which lies just inside the entrance to the antiquities site, directly on the road along the eastern bank of the Nile, eight-and-a-half kilometres south of Minya. The Elephantine pyramid may be seen from a distance along the usual tour route around the island of Elephantine and its museums.

THE PREHISTORY OF THE PYRAMID

What may well be the oldest surviving Egyptian royal burial is Tomb 100 at Hierakonpolis. Among the large tombs found at this site, which seems to have been the capital of the first rulers of southern Egypt, there is one whose main room, a brick-lined cutting in the desert surface, was adorned with scenes of boats and hunting. This earliest known decorated tomb may have been made for a 'proto-pharaoh' of prehistoric times, *c.* 3300 BC.

Above: The earliest burials in Egypt were simple pits in the desert, the body interred in a crouched position. The dry conditions have sometimes dried out the corpses to produce natural mummies, as seen here.

From just a little later, shortly before Egypt was unified around 3000 BC, comes the first sepulchre that we know to be that of a king – at Abydos, later to become one of the most sacred of all Egyptian cities of the dead. Here lay the ancient cemetery of Umm el-Qaab, at the mouth of a valley leading up into the Western Desert; its early choice as a burial place may have resulted from its being regarded as a gateway to the West, the home of the dead. This first tomb, known as U-j, is identical in construction with Hierakonpolis' Tomb 100, although far larger, with a dozen rooms. It is the direct ancestor of a whole series of similar tombs built there by the kings of the First Dynasty, the first rulers of the whole country.

First Dynasty Developments

As the dynasty continued, the substructures at Umm el-Qaab became more elaborate, the most important innovation being the introduction of a stairway entrance during the reign of King Den. Previously, the tomb-chamber had had to be left unroofed until after the burial, thus postponing the construction of the

CHRONOLOGY OF THE PREDYNASTIC & ARCHAIC PERIODS

PREDYNASTIC PERIOD
BADARIAN CULTURE
(5000–4000)

NAQADA I (AMRATIAN) CULTURE
(4000–3500)

NAQADA II (GERZIAN) CULTURE
(3500–3150)

PROTODYNASTIC PERIOD
NAQADA III CULTURE
(3150–3000)

BLACK TOPPED RED
POT FROM ABYDOS
TOMB, 1730

RED-LINED
POT

CARVED
MACE HEAD
FROM REIGN
OF KING
SCORPION

superstructure. Now, this element could be built in advance. Although virtually no Umm el-Qaab superstructure has survived, a key element was a pair of stelae that marked out an offering place, apparently on the east side of the tomb. There may also have been a low mound directly over the burial chamber; however, this may not have projected above ground level.

This modest installation was only one part of the arrangements for the sustenance of the royal spirit. A wadi (dried-up watercourse) leads from Umm el-Qaab towards the edge of the desert and the ancient town of Abydos, and on its margins, nearly two kilometres from the royal tombs, a series of huge brick enclosures was constructed, each partnering a tomb at Umm el-Qaab. Although almost all have been destroyed, it seems that they each contained a chapel, and perhaps temporary wooden buildings as well. At least one was

Above: The First Dynasty royal cemetery was at Umm el-Qaab, a low mound at Abydos that lies at the mouth of a wadi – dried-up watercourse – leading into the high Western Desert. This may have been regarded as a gateway to the realm of the dead, and therefore an appropriate place to be buried.

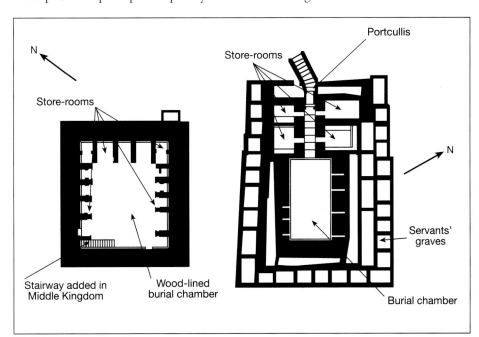

N

Store-rooms

Portcullis

Store-rooms

N

Stairway added in Middle Kingdom

Wood-lined burial chamber

Servants' graves

Burial chamber

Left: The substructures of the tombs at Umm el-Qaab comprised brick-lined cuttings in the desert gravel. That of Djer (O) had no means of access other than through its ceiling; the later tomb of Qaa (Q) has, in contrast, a stairway from outside the perimeter.

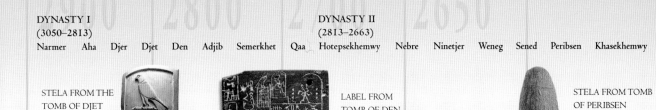

2900   2800   2700   2650

DYNASTY I
(3050–2813)
Narmer   Aha   Djer   Djet   Den   Adjib   Semerkhet   Qaa

DYNASTY II
(2813–2663)
Hotepsekhemwy   Nebre   Ninetjer   Weneg   Sened   Peribsen   Khasekhemwy

STELA FROM THE
TOMB OF DJET

LABEL FROM
TOMB OF DEN

STELA FROM TOMB
OF PERIBSEN

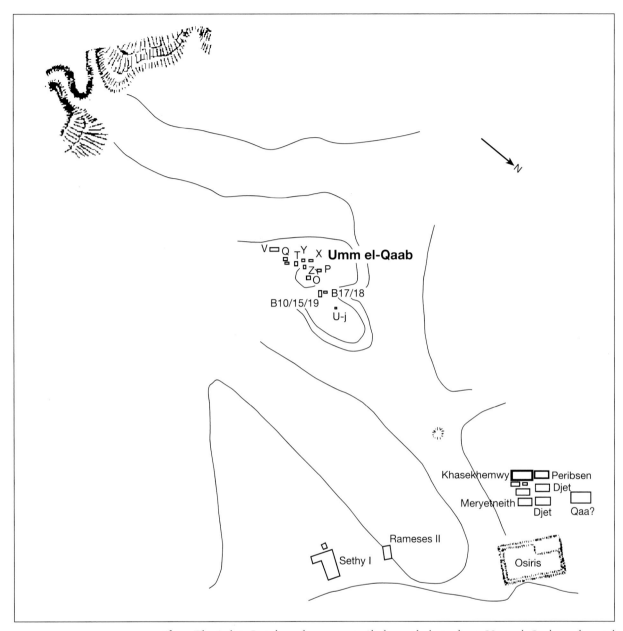

Above: *The Archaic Period royal cemetery at Abydos, with the tombs at Umm el-Qaab supplemented by the funerary enclosures near the edge of the desert and the temple of Osiris. The Umm el-Qaab tombs are as follows: O, Djer; P, Peribsen; Q, Qaa; T, Den; U, Semerkhet; V, Khasekhemwy; X, Anedjib; Y, Meryetneith; Z, Djet; B10/15/19, Hor-Aha; B17/18, Narmer; U-j, 'Scorpion'.*

equipped with a fleet of real wooden boats, while most were surrounded – like the Umm el-Qaab tombs – with the graves of members of the royal household. At least some of these seem to have been filled at the same time as that of the king, indicating a custom of human sacrifice that was to die out before the building of the first pyramid. It is possible that these enclosures were dismantled relatively soon after a king's death, when the structure to honour the next monarch was begun. This may explain why the only example still standing is that of the last king to be buried in the area, the Second Dynasty's last monarch, Khasekhemwy.

The Second Dynasty

The advent of the Second Dynasty around 2800 BC led to an important change in royal burial arrangements, with its founder, Hotepsekhemwy, abandoning Umm el-Qaab in favour of Saqqara, over 300 kilometres to the north. This site, on a ridge over-looking the city of Memphis, was the principal cemetery of Egypt's capital, founded at the beginning of the First Dynasty, and already housed the tombs of many of the nobility of the time. The location chosen by the king was some 1,500 metres to the south of these sepulchres, reflecting the 'cordon sanitaire' that separated the ruler and the ruled in death for the first four centuries of Egypt's united history. The substructure of the tomb is of a wholly new type, tunnelled out of the bedrock and many times larger than anything that had come before, with around 80 chambers and a series of portcullis slabs blocking the entrance corridor.

The whole area above Hotepsekhemwy's tomb was destroyed when the pyramid of Unas (see pages 72–3) was built nearly 500 years later, but the slightly more recent example of Ninetjer shows a superstructure in two distinct parts. The northern element seems to have been an area some 19 or 20 metres deep, intended for funerary ceremonies; floored with a layer of clay, it lay above the outer passages and chambers of the tomb. Beyond this, to the south, was a rock

Above: The monumental part of the Abydos royal tombs lay closer to the edge of desert, the only preserved example being the Second Dynasty example of Khasekhemwy.

Below: This detailed view of Khasekhemwy's monument shows the massive panelled enclosure wall.

'step', apparently marking the spot where the substantial part of the superstructure may have begun.

Like the royal tombs of Abydos, Hotepsekhemwy's tomb also included a rectangular enclosure, although in this case it lay in the desert beyond the burial place, at the end of a wadi that seems to have been the ancient ceremonial route to the new royal necropolis (see 'D' on aerial image below). The enclosure that seems to have belonged to the king had been constructed by piling up desert gravel to delineate an area considerably bigger than any of the brick enclosures at Abydos. Another enclosure, known as the Gisr el-Mudir, and perhaps belonging to Ninetjer, lies a little to the southwest, and had stone walls — a candidate for the earliest major stone-building work in the world.

At least three other Second Dynasty kings appear to have been buried at Saqqara, but Peribsen opted to move back to Abydos, with a tomb that closely reflects First Dynasty norms in both size and construction. Civil war appears to have followed Peribsen's tenure of the throne, and the only further royal tomb known from the dynasty is that of the war's victor, Khasekhemwy, at Abydos.

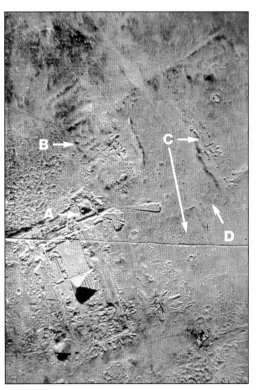

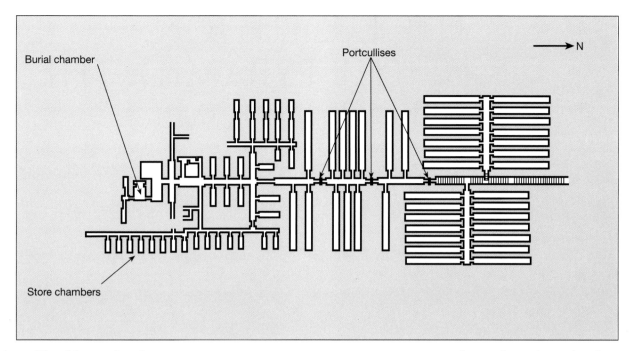

Burial chamber

Portcullises

→ N

Store chambers

Khasekhemwy's substructure appears to represent an attempt to marry the labyrinthine design of Hotepsekhemwy's tomb with the conditions at Umm el-Qaab, where tunnelling was impracticable causing the chambers to be built in a cutting. Khasekhemwy's enclosure, situated alongside those of his predecessors near the desert edge, is by far the best preserved. Most of the exterior wall still survives, as do traces of buildings within, including a series of basins of uncertain purpose. The traces of one of these were for a time misinterpreted as those of a brick-sheathed mound.

In Egyptian cosmology, creation took place on a mound that rose above the waters of creation – in the same way as newly fertile land appeared as the annual Nile inundation subsided. Thus the 'primaeval' mound could play a role in the essential act of creation that was the rebirth of the soul after death. Such a mound had been placed above the burial apartments of royal and private tombs of the First Dynasty, and it is not improbable that this motif would provide the point of origin for the development of the pyramid at the beginning of the Third Dynasty.

At the end of the Second Dynasty, the basic form of the royal tomb had been set for some four centuries as a burial complex of chambers topped by a monument, along with an associated rectangular enclosure for ritual structures situated some distance away.

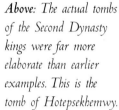

Above: The actual tombs of the Second Dynasty kings were far more elaborate than earlier examples. This is the tomb of Hotepsekhemwy.

Left: Two kings of the Second Dynasty were buried at Umm el-Qaab; the first was Peribsen, one of whose stelae is shown here. The largely erased figure at the top is the god Seth, to whom the king seems to have been devoted, rather than the traditional royal god, Horus.

THE EVOLUTION OF THE PYRAMID: THE OLD KINGDOM

Below*: The Step Pyramid complex of Djoser in Saqqara was the first royal funerary monument to be built entirely from stone.*

The beginning of the Third Dynasty marked a major conceptual and technological leap forward, compared with the previous dynasty. This included the erection of the first known pyramid, the precursor of a series that would not come to an end until nearly 3,000 years later.

CHRONOLOGY OF THE OLD KINGDOM

DYNASTY III						DYNASTY IV				
Djoser	Sanakhte	Sekhemkhet	Khaba	Huni	Seneferu	Khufu	Djedefre	Khaefre	Menkaure	Shepseskaf

STEP PYRAMID OF DJOSER

STATUETTE OF KHUFU

STATUE OF KHAEFRE

MENKAURE, GODDESS HATHOR AND GOD OF THEBES

The Third Dynasty

Khasekhemwy was succeeded by the founder of the Third Dynasty, a ruler known to history as Djoser. This king was long remembered, and his importance was signalled by his name being written uniquely in red in a later list of monarchs. Millennia later, the fourth-century BC Egyptian historian Manetho recorded that his reign saw the 'invent[ion] of the art of building in hewn stone'. Although this is not strictly true,

in view of the known stone monuments of the Second Dynasty, it is clear that the reign witnessed an extraordinary advance in building technology.

Sadly, our knowledge of the rest of the Third Dynasty is very sketchy, with even the royal succession uncertain. Much of what has been reconstructed is based on the unfinished tombs that have been identified around the Memphite necropolis.

Above: The Step Pyramid enclosure in essence turns the earlier brick enclosure into stone; this is its entrance.

DJOSER'S PYRAMID (STEP PYRAMID)

The Step Pyramid dominates the site of Saqqara, dwarfing the surrounding monuments, and rising in six levels to a summit some 60 metres above its foundations. Built entirely of quarried blocks of stone, it is generally regarded as the first large stone building in the world. It was begun as a low, square structure, which was then enlarged into a four-stepped pyramid, and then into the final six-stepped rectangular structure. It lay in the centre of an extraordinary complex of stone buildings, enclosed by a panelled stone wall, the western part of which incorporated a probable royal tomb of the Second Dynasty. The building material apart, the wall has much in common with the brick examples at Abydos. Like them, it was entered from a gateway at the southern end of the east side, leading into an open courtyard containing elements associated with the ritual race that formed part of the royal jubilee (*Heb-sed*) ceremonies. A complex of shrines in the adjacent 'Heb-sed Court' were also associated with these activities, and many of the other structures within the pyramid enclosure also seem to be related to either jubilee or coronation ceremonies. A temple on the north side of the pyramid follows a plan known (in private tombs) since the First Dynasty, and included a statue of the king enclosed in a windowless room known as a *serdab*. A

MODERN DESIGNATION: L.XXXII; el-Haram el-Mudarrag; the Step Pyramid
LOCATION: Saqqara
DATE: *c.* 2663–2643 BC
OWNER: Netjerkhet Djoser
BASIS OF ATTRIBUTION: Inscriptions within sub-structure and complex
DIMENSIONS: Base 121 x 109 metres; height 60 metres

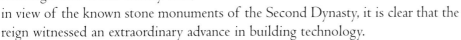

DYNASTY V									DYNASTY VI				
Userkaf	Sahure	Neferirkare	Shepseskare	Neferefre	Niuserre	Menkauhor	Isesi	Unas	Teti	Pepy I	Nemtyemsaf I	Pepy II	Nemtyemsaf II

A SCRIBE OF DYNASTY V

RELIEF OF MENKAUHOR

SARCOPHAGUS OF QUEEN ANKHENESPEPY IV

Above: Elaborate chapel buildings lie within the Step Pyramid, all based on temporary wooden structures that were here transformed into limestone buildings.

Below: Plan of the Step Pyramid enclosure, showing the key elements.

mastaba was built into the south enclosure wall, with chambers mirroring those of the pyramid. This seems to be the direct ancestor of the later subsidiary pyramids.

The entrance to the tomb chambers lay within the temple. These centred on a burial chamber constructed at the bottom of a vertical shaft. This room was unusual in being entered via a hole in the roof, blocked by a piece of stone similar to a sink plug. A series of galleries surrounded the burial chamber, some decorated with blue faience plaques, others also with reliefs of the king – the first and last time a king would be shown in his own tomb until the New Kingdom. Under one side of the pyramid was a series of shaft tombs intended for members of the king's family.

The earliest modern explorers found parts of one or more mummies within the pyramid, and a number of other portions of a body were found in the burial chamber in the 1930s. Their age is uncertain; the location of the finds suggests that they are contemporary with the pyramid and thus those of the king, but recent carbon-14 tests have thrown doubt on this supposition. These remains apart, non-architectural material recovered from the pyramid proper has been limited to a wooden box

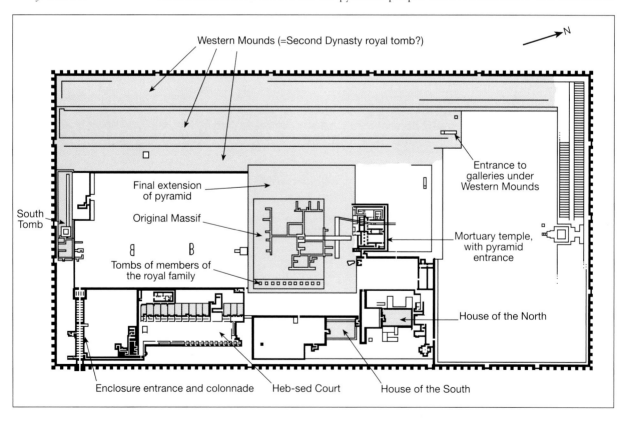

Western Mounds (=Second Dynasty royal tomb?)

N

Final extension of pyramid

Original Massif

Entrance to galleries under Western Mounds

South Tomb

Tombs of members of the royal family

Mortuary temple, with pyramid entrance

House of the North

Enclosure entrance and colonnade   Heb-sed Court   House of the South bearing the king's name. The tombs of the royal family under the east side of the pyramid revealed a number of alabaster sarcophagi, one containing human remains, seal impressions and large numbers of stone vessels, many dating back to the First and Second Dynasties.

Apart from the pyramid at its centre, Djoser's complex was in essence a simple combination of the formerly separate elements of the royal tomb into one unit, eternalized in stone. The union of the burial

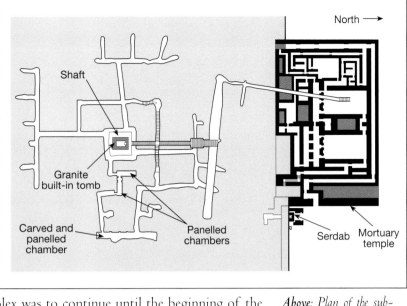

Above: Plan of the substructure and mortuary temple of the Step Pyramid.

place with the complete cult complex was to continue until the beginning of the New Kingdom, although with many changes and developments.

The Step Pyramid is the only such monument whose architect is known. He was Imhotep, Chancellor of Egypt; his name appears on the base of a statue of Djoser from the pyramid complex – a unique honour for a commoner. During the Late Period, Imhotep was deified as a god of medicine, and as such was the subject of many small metal votive figures found in the Sacred Animal Necropolis, north of the Step Pyramid. Imhotep's tomb was probably in this area.

Principal Explorations
The first 'archaeological' investigations were made by the Egyptians of the Twenty-sixth Dynasty, who drove a new entrance passage into the long-plundered monument, apparently to some of the reliefs within. Although the pyramid had been seen by travellers, the first modern penetration of the substructure was probably by Segato and Minutoli in 1820. Perring carried out a more detailed investigation in 1839, but it was not until 1924–29 that Firth (continued by Quibell and Lauer) began comprehensive excavation work. Many of the buildings have been reconstructed, but several areas remain to be fully investigated.

Left: The Step Pyramid is the only such monument to have an extensively decorated substructure, a number of rooms being lined with faience tiles and given inscribed doorways.

EL-DEIR AT ABU ROWASH

MODERN DESIGNATION: El-Deir

LOCATION: Abu Rowash

DATE: c. 2643–2633 BC

OWNER: Sanakhte Nebka?

BASIS OF ATTRIBUTION: The king lacks a known tomb, and the monument's design seems appropriate to a royal tomb of this date.

DIMENSIONS: Base 20 x 20 metres; height 4.15+ metres

Djoser's successor seems to have been Sanakhte – until recently thought to have been his predecessor. It is possible that a mysterious monument at Abu Rowash may be his tomb. It was a great brick enclosure, probably 280 by 150 metres, with a solid brick structure in the centre, built upon a rocky knoll, and still over 4 metres high in 1902. Early Old Kingdom pottery was found there, and the scale and form of the monument strongly suggest that it was a royal tomb of the Second or Third Dynasty. As it was only after Djoser that royal tombs are known to have moved away from Saqqara within the Memphite region, the latter date is more likely. Sanakhte is the leading candidate as he would otherwise have no tomb.

Principal Explorations

First noticed by Vyse in 1837, and excavated by Palenque in 1902 and by Makramallah in 1931, the latter exploration being a rescue excavation following the installation of a drainage pipe. No further work on the site is recorded. Additional damage is known to have resulted from irrigation schemes.

Right Plan of El-Deir, which may represent the tomb of Sanakhte.

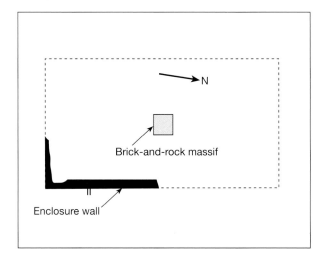

Brick-and-rock massif

Enclosure wall

Right: Abu Rowash overlooks the beginning of the Delta, and just at this point, at the top left of this view, lies El-Deir.

SEKHEMKHET'S PYRAMID

MODERN DESIGNATION: Unfinished Pyramid

LOCATION: Saqqara

DATE: c. 2633–2626 BC

OWNER: Sekhemkhet Djoserti

BASIS OF ATTRIBUTION: The king is named on seal-impressions within the substructure.

DIMENSIONS: Base 120 x 120 metres

Although unfinished, possibly due to the early death of the king, this monument seems to have been intended to be similar to Djoser's, with a large panelled enclosure. The enclosure was enlarged at least once before being abandoned, and had what was presumably intended to be a ritual mastaba tomb in its southern part. This was, however, used for the burial of a two-year-old child, probably during the Third Dynasty.

In the centre of the enclosure are the remains of a seven-stepped pyramid, whose construction had been abandoned at an early stage. Its entrance lay in the centre of the north face, the approach ramp cutting through the terrace upon which the mortuary temple would have been built. Interestingly, two attempts had been made to cut the subterranean corridors. The first was abandoned after 10 metres; the floor of the ramp was then raised and a new cutting begun. This was carried forward and extended 72 metres into the bedrock. A little beyond the entrance, a doorway was cut in the right wall, from which a right-angled passage led back northward to give access to a long U-shaped corridor,

off which lay 132 small storage chambers. These chambers held a large number of both finished and unfinished stone vessels, among which were the seal impressions that bore Sekhemkhet's name.

Above: The entrance to the pyramid of Sekhemkhet; the filling around it was intended as the foundations of the mortuary temple, but this was never built.

Beyond the doorway leading to the store-rooms, the roof of the main passage was interrupted by the bottom of a vertical shaft. This penetrated up through the superstructure, and may have been intended for the lowering of a portcullis slab; this arrangement is common in tombs of the period. However, no such slab was found, although a set of gold jewellery was found buried in the floor of the corridor directly below it.

The corridor also contained three intact (although rebuilt) blockings, while the roughly hewn burial chamber contained an alabaster sarcophagus of unique form – it had a sliding panel at one end sealed with plaster – and the remains of what was interpreted as a funerary wreath on top of the box. Unfortunately, the sarcophagus proved to be empty, with no trace of a body anywhere in the pyramid.

Principal Explorations

The site was identified by aerial photographs, and excavated by Goneim from 1951. After Goneim's death, further work was carried out by Lauer, beginning in 1964.

Below: Plan of the unfinished pyramid complex of Sekhemkhet.

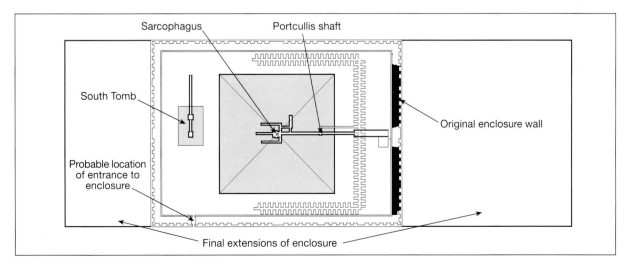

MODERN DESIGNATION:
L.XIV; Layer Pyramid

LOCATION: Zawiyet el-Aryan

DATE: *c.* 2626–2621 BC

OWNER: Khaba

BASIS OF ATTRIBUTION:
Inscribed bowls found
in a nearby tomb; the
pyramid is dated typo-
logically directly after
Sekhemkhet's

DIMENSIONS: Base 84 x
84 metres

*Below: Plan and sections
of the Layer Pyramid.*

KHABA'S PYRAMID (LAYER PYRAMID)

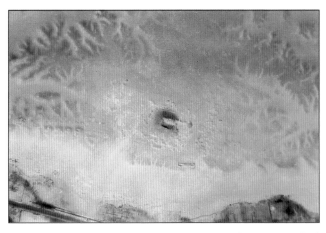

This monument lies on the edge of a steep incline from the desert down to the edge of the fields – a rather different location from earlier monuments and one unsuitable for the kind of rectangular enclosure found around them. It may thus be at this point that the first major shift in the architecture of the pyramid complex occurred, with a much less elaborate cult installation (mortuary temple, causeway, etc.) centred on the eastern side, and some form of ramp leading down to the edge of the desert – blocks have been seen here that might have formed part of a valley building. Such an arrangement might explain the pyramid's novel position on the very edge of the desert.

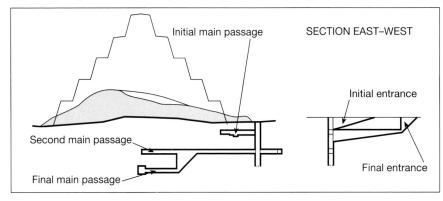

The pyramid derives its modern name, the 'Layer Pyramid', from the large breach in the north side that has revealed a neat section of its internal structure. This is of the same kind as seen in the Step Pyramid and Sekhemkhet's Pyramid: a series of facings whose successively reduced height produced steps.

The design of the substructure shows it to be almost certainly the direct successor of Sekhemkhet's monument. It has the same U-shaped set of store galleries, albeit with store-rooms on one side only, and a wholly tunnelled substructure. However, it demonstrates a number of advances over the older monument. The latter's store galleries had been approached via an awkward passage that doubled back on the entrance gallery, which would have made access difficult. In the Layer Pyramid, the entrance ramp was

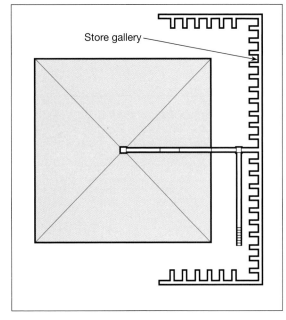

Above: The Layer Pyramid was probably the first royal tomb to break away from Archaic prototypes by abandoning the massive rectangular shape. The pyramid itself was 84 metres square. The cavity in the north face was created by early hunters seeking the entrance to the burial chamber.

turned through 90 degrees so that at the bottom of the ramp a right turn would lead direct to the store-rooms, and a left turn would lead to the burial chamber.

This basic conception was maintained through a number of modifications, all apparently intended to place the burial chamber still deeper underground, perhaps because of poor-quality rock at the highest level. Whatever the reason, galleries at two successive levels were abandoned before the final burial chamber was cut, and were apparently left unused.

Principal Explorations

First investigated in 1881 by Maspero, who located the entrance stairway but failed to enter the substructure; the first person in modern times to do that was Barsanti, in 1900. Reisner and Fisher worked on the site in 1910, but concentrated on the clearance of the tombs that lay around the pyramid, one of which (Z.500) contained stone bowls naming Khaba.

THE BRICK PYRAMID AT ABU ROWASH

This structure lies something over a kilometre south of El-Deir. Today, it appears at first sight to be no more than a rock knoll at the southern end of Abu Rowash village. However, in the 1840s, it was surmounted by various masses of mud brick. Though these have since disappeared, the emplacements for them are still clear, consistent with it having been the core of a pyramid of this material. High up on the north side, a passageway descends to an entirely rock-cut burial chamber, a method of chamber construction not found after the early Fourth Dynasty. The high entrance is also a feature of the period.

Although reverting to a much more ancient building material than the preceding monuments – brick was not used again for a pyramid until the Middle Kingdom – this was by far the biggest pyramid yet begun, and the fourth largest pyramid of all time. Construction from brick would seem at first glance to be a retrograde step, but it is conceivable that this well-tried medium was used in order to get the building completed more quickly. This could also account for the monument's proximity to the cultivation (i.e. cultivated land): to allow easy access to the bricks' raw material.

The pyramid seems never to have been finished, and by the end of the Old Kingdom enough of the rock core had been exposed by the removal of bricks to allow the construction of tombs cut into it.

The distant memory of a giant brick pyramid of the Old Kingdom may lie behind the Greek historian Herodotus' story of the

MODERN DESIGNATION: L.I; Brick Pyramid
LOCATION: Abu Rowash
DATE: c. 2621–2597 BC
OWNER: Huni (?)
BASIS OF ATTRIBUTION: Typological position (see text) and the historical placement of the king seem to coincide.
DIMENSIONS: Base 215 x 215 metres

Below: The Brick Pyramid at Abu Rowash still retained significant parts of its brickwork when drawn by Lepsius' team in 1842–43.

Right: By the 20th century, all that was left of the Brick Pyramid at Abu Rowash was the bare core of a natural rock knoll.

Right: Reconstructed section and plan of the Brick Pyramid.

legendary Asychis, 'the successor of Mykerinos [Menkaure], who… wishing to go one better than his predecessors, built a pyramid of brick to commemorate his reign, and on it cut an inscription in stone to the following effect: "Do not compare me to my disadvantage with the stone pyramids. I surpass them as far as does Zeus [i.e. Amun] the other gods. They pushed a pole to the bottom of a lake, and the mud which stuck on it they collected and made into bricks. That is how they built me."

Principal Explorations
Drawn and described by Lepsius' team in 1842–3. Rediscovered by Swelim, who undertook a preliminary survey in 1985–6.

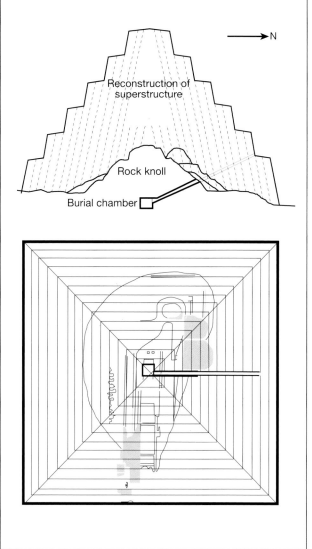

The Fourth Dynasty

The Fourth Dynasty, beginning with Seneferu around 2600 BC, marks the last part of the experimental phase of pyramid design and construction. During the dynasty's one and a quarter centuries, pyramids reached and passed the zenith of size and quality of building; there then appeared the first examples of the 'standard' pyramid complex, examples of which were still to be found as late as the Twelfth Dynasty, eight centuries later. The Fourth Dynasty saw the change from the step pyramid to the 'true' form, i.e. with smooth sides: in Egyptian, △

The reason for this change has been much debated, but the consensus is that the true pyramid was a solar symbol, representing the sun's rays striking down from the sky. This fits well with the prominence of the sun cult during the remaining part of the Old Kingdom, and it is likely that, in addition to any benefits that would accrue from being buried under such a manifestation of the sun, there was some conception of the rays providing a 'ramp' to the heavens.

The Fourth Dynasty opens with the greatest pyramid builder of them all, Seneferu, who during his half-century on the throne seems to have erected no fewer than ten of these structures!

SENEFERU'S FIRST PYRAMID

 *'Seneferu endures'*

Seneferu's pyramid at Meidum is the southernmost of all the major pyramids of the Old Kingdom, presumably built near a residence of its owner. It was begun as a seven-stepped pyramid, which was then enlarged and converted to an eight-stepped one. Finally, probably after a break, it was converted into a true pyramid. Later stone robbery caused some of the outer layers of the upper part to collapse,

Below: The pyramid at Meidum represents the transition between step and true pyramids; parts of all its building phases may be seen on today's ruin. The causeway runs from a small mortuary temple towards the valley building.

MODERN DESIGNATION: L.LXV; Haram el-Kaddeb (False Pyramid)
LOCATION: Meidum
DATE: *c.* 2597–2547 BC
OWNER: Seneferu
BASIS OF ATTRIBUTION: Date of the adjacent private tombs, its design and later tourist graffiti. Earlier ideas that it might have been begun by Huni and completed by Seneferu are now generally rejected
DIMENSIONS: Base 144 x 144 metres; height 92 metres

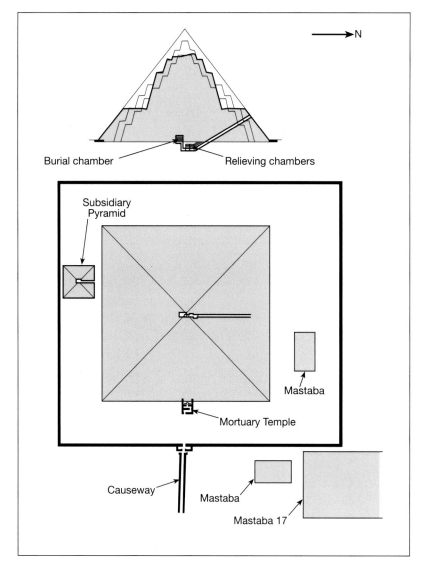

Burial chamber — Relieving chambers

Subsidiary Pyramid

Mastaba

Mortuary Temple

Causeway

Mastaba

Mastaba 17

Above: Section and plan of the Meidum pyramid.

leaving the true pyramid intact at the bottom, together with a tower-like structure which preserves the fifth and sixth steps of the eight-stepped version.

A small mortuary chapel was built on the east side, with two unfinished stelae and an offering table in the sanctuary. Although the line of the causeway survives, the valley building has never been excavated. A subsidiary pyramid, now destroyed, stood in front of the south face of the main pyramid.

The substructure was constructed partly in the pyramid core and partly in a cutting in the bedrock. The burial chamber was entered from below and corbel-roofed. To relieve pressure on flat roofs, corbelled cavities were constructed above the antechambers and the lower part of the descending corridor. No sarcophagus was included and the pyramid was probably not used for a burial.

Principal Explorations

The exterior of the pyramid was described by a number of early travellers and investigators, including Perring on 29 October 1839, before being entered by Maspero in 1882. Excavations were carried out by Petrie in 1892, 1910 and 1912, and then by Rowe in 1929–30. Finally, El-Khouli worked here in 1984, as did a Supreme Council for Antiquities team at the end of the 1990s, the latter discovering the relieving chambers.

SENEFERU'S SECOND PYRAMID (BENT PYRAMID)

 *'Seneferu appears–South'*

This was the first pyramid to be begun as a true pyramid, although still employing inwardly-sloping masonry as found in step pyramids. The latter feature has contributed to its being externally the best preserved of all pyramids. It appears that structural problems manifested themselves in the substructure part way through its construction, leading to the angle – and so weight – of the upper part of the pyramid being reduced and thus creating its distinctive shape; the upper part was built from horizontal, rather than inwardly-sloping, courses.

A small mortuary temple was built on the east side, and a causeway led to the valley building at the top of a wadi leading down to the desert edge. The mortuary temple, the first surviving example of such a building, was extensively decorated with reliefs and statuary. A subsidiary pyramid lay south of the main pyramid, with a chapel to its east.

The Bent Pyramid's original substructure was similar to that of the Meidum pyramid, except that the shaft leading to the burial chamber was replaced by a steep staircase. However, a unique additional set of corridors and a chamber, approached from the west, was built within the pyramid masonry itself. This was added following the structural failures within the original complex. No sarcophagus was included in either complex and the pyramid was probably not used for a burial.

MODERN DESIGNATION:
L.LVI; Bent Pyramid
LOCATION: Dahshur
DATE: *c.* 2597–2547 BC
OWNER: Seneferu
BASIS OF ATTRIBUTION:
Name appears on inscriptions throughout pyramid complex
DIMENSIONS: Base 188 x 188 metres; height 105 metres

Left: *The small mortuary temple is on the east side of the Bent Pyramid.*

Below: *To the north-east of the Bent Pyramid lie the remains of the valley building.*

Above: The Bent Pyramid's valley building contained a number of statues of the king; this one wears the White Crown.

Right: Sections and plan of the Bent Pyramid complex.

MODERN DESIGNATION: L.XLIX; Red Pyramid; North Stone Pyramid
LOCATION: Dahshur
DATE: *c.* 2597–2547 BC
OWNER: Seneferu
BASIS OF ATTRIBUTION: Quarry marks on blocks and later inscriptions
DIMENSIONS: Base 220 x 220 metres; height 105 metres

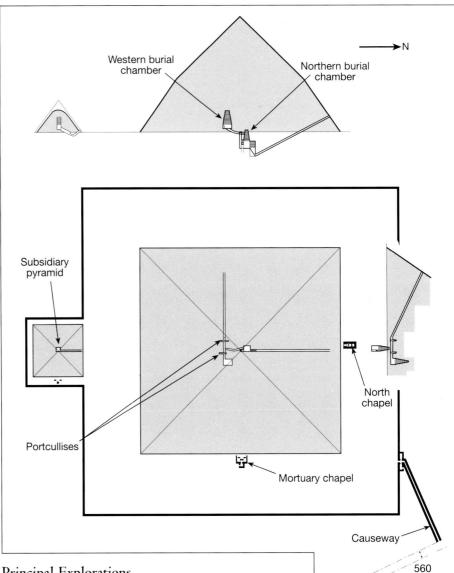

Western burial chamber

Northern burial chamber

N

Subsidiary pyramid

Portcullises

North chapel

Mortuary chapel

Causeway

560 metres

Valley building

Principal Explorations

The earliest documented entries are by Wood in 1750 and by Davison in 1763; Davison penetrated some 70–80 metres into the north corridor. The inner part and western complex were first entered by Perring in September 1839, and fully cleared and excavated by Hussein and then Fakhry between 1947 and 1955.

SENEFERU'S THIRD PYRAMID (RED PYRAMID)

'Seneferu Appears'

This, the final pyramid built for Seneferu, was constructed entirely using the lower angle that was applied to the upper part of the Bent Pyramid.

A rather more elaborate mortuary temple than those of Seneferu's previous two pyramids was provided, but a proper causeway seems never to have been constructed. The form of the valley building remains unknown, although what seemed

Above: The Red Pyramid at Dahshur, built uniformly at the lower angle used on the upper part of the Bent Pyramid.

to be parts of it were noticed during the 19th century. Likewise, no subsidiary pyramid has been found, although the pyramidion (cap-stone) of such a monument – too steeply angled for the Red Pyramid itself – has been discovered.

The substructure was built at ground level within the body of the pyramid. It comprised three spectacular corbelled rooms, the third entered from high up in the wall of the second, clearly for concealment. A sarcophagus may have been built into the floor, and fragments of a mummy, probably of Seneferu himself, were found in the pyramid.

Principal Explorations

The first recorded entries are by an anonymous Scot in 1657, and by Melton in 1661; the pyramid was subsequently surveyed by Perring in 1839 and the interior cleared by Hussein in 1947. The pyramid has been excavated by Stadelmann since 1977.

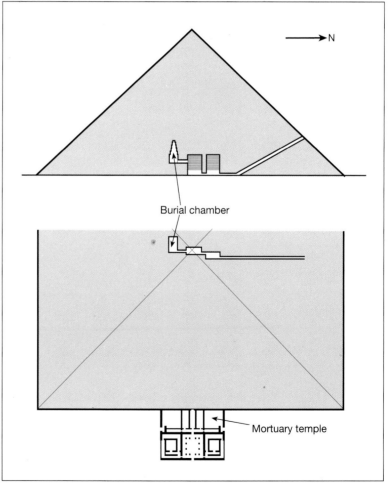

Above: Section and plan of the Red (Seneferu's third) Pyramid.

PYRAMID AT SEILA

MODERN DESIGNATION:
El-Qalah

LOCATION: Seila

DATE: c. 2597–2547 BC

OWNER: Seneferu

BASIS OF ATTRIBUTION:
Stelae bearing the name
of the king

DIMENSIONS: Base 31 x
31 metres

A series of small step pyramids, all apparently without any original substructure, are spread through Middle and Upper Egypt. Nothing is known of their purpose, although their positions, dotted along the Nile, might suggest the marking of some kind of royal tour. The small step pyramid at Seila is in a prominent position, at an elevation of 124 metres on top of the Gebel el-Rus, commanding a view west into the Fayoum and east over the Nile valley. A small brick chapel with an altar, statue and stelae bearing the name of its founder stands on its east side, with another chapel on the north face.

Principal Explorations

Summarily examined by Petrie, Borchardt and others; finally cleared by a team from Brigham Young University, USA, in association with Swelim, in the 1980s.

PYRAMID AT ZAWIYET SULTAN

MODERN DESIGNATION:
None

LOCATION: Zawiyet
Sultan (site also known
as Zawiyet el-Maiyitin
or Zawiyet el-Amwat)

DATE: c. 2597–2547 BC

OWNER: Seneferu (?)

BASIS OF ATTRIBUTION:
Similarities to the pyra-
mid at Seila

DIMENSIONS: Base 22.4
x 22.4 metres

One of the series of small step pyramids of obscure purpose, it lies close to the major ancient site of Hebenu and is, unusually, on the east bank of the Nile.

Principal Explorations

First examined by Weill in 1911 and by Lauer in 1962.

Right: Seven small pyramids were built south of the Memphite necropolis around the beginning of the Fourth Dynasty, possibly all by Seneferu. This is the example at Zawiyet Sultan in Middle Egypt.

PYRAMID AT NUBT

One of the series of small step pyramids of obscure purpose. A pit was found below the structure, but may not be associated with its original construction.

Principal Explorations
Partly cleared by Petrie in 1896.

MODERN DESIGNATION: Qurn el-Shair

LOCATION: Nubt (El-Zawayda, Naqada)

DATE: c. 2597–2547 BC

OWNER: Seneferu (?)

BASIS OF ATTRIBUTION: Similarities to the
pyramid at Seila

DIMENSIONS: Base 18 x 18 metres

PYRAMID AT SINKI

Another of this series of small step pyramids; this one was never completed and still retains its constructional ramps.

Principal Explorations

Noted by Maspero and Wilbour in 1883, and then re-identified by Swelim on 27 October 1977; excavated by Swelim and Dreyer in 1980.

MODERN DESIGNATION: None

LOCATION: Sinki (Nag Ahmed Khalifa, Abydos)

DATE: c. 2597–2547 BC

OWNER: Seneferu (?)

BASIS OF ATTRIBUTION: Similarities to the pyramid at Seila

DIMENSIONS: Base 18.5 x 18.5 metres

PYRAMID AT EL-KULA

Until recently, this pyramid was the best-known of the series of small step pyramids; this monument is odd in having its corners oriented to the points of the compass.

Principal Explorations

The pyramid was visited by Rifaud sometime between 1816 and 1826, and by Vyse in 1836, and then examined by Maspero in 1882. This work resulted in the removal of blocks from the north side. A further investigation was made by Capart in 1946.

MODERN DESIGNATION: None

LOCATION: El-Kula (Nag el-Miamariya, Edfu-North)

DATE: c. 2597–2547 BC

OWNER: Seneferu (?)

BASIS OF ATTRIBUTION: Similarities to the pyramid at Seila

DIMENSIONS: Base 18.6 x 18.6 metres

Left: The three-stepped pyramid at El-Kula. As with the other small pyramids, no trace of a substructure has ever been found, despite several investigations.

PYRAMID AT EL-GHENIMIA

Unlike the preceding small step pyramids, this example is of sandstone, reflecting the local geology.

Principal Explorations

Identified by Aly around 1980.

MODERN DESIGNATION: Abu Sinnah

LOCATION: El-Ghenimia (Edfu-South)

DATE: c. 2597–2547 BC

OWNER: Seneferu (?)

BASIS OF ATTRIBUTION: Similarities to the pyramid at Seila

DIMENSIONS: Base 22 x 22 metres

PYRAMID AT ELEPHANTINE

MODERN DESIGNATION:
None
LOCATION: Elephantine
DATE: *c.* 2597–2547 BC
OWNER: Seneferu (?)
BASIS OF ATTRIBUTION:
Similarities to the pyramid at Seila
DIMENSIONS: Base 25 x 25 metres

This small step pyramid was built of local granite. The Old Kingdom element of the city lay 120 metres to the south-east, but later expansion has placed the pyramid within the ancient settlement area known as Elephantine.

A granite cone was found nearby bearing the name of Huni, which has frequently led to the pyramid being assigned to him.

Principal Explorations

Initially misidentified as the foundations of a Jewish temple early in the 20th century, its true status was recognized by Dreyer in 1979.

Right: The pyramid at Elephantine is now almost entirely hidden among later buildings, but is visible in the centre of this view.

KHUFU'S PYRAMID (GREAT PYRAMID)

  'Horizon of Khufu'

MODERN DESIGNATION:
L.IV; G I; Great Pyramid
LOCATION: Giza
DATE: *c.* 2547–2524 BC
OWNER: Khufu
BASIS OF ATTRIBUTION:
Quarry marks inside pyramid; numerous monuments of family and officials in surrounding cemeteries
DIMENSIONS: Base 230 x 230 metres; height 146 metres

This is the so-called Great Pyramid, the largest of all the pyramids. A mortuary temple was built on the east side, directly south of which was the subsidiary pyramid. A causeway led towards the valley building, some elements of which have been detected under modern buildings below the desert escarpment. A number of boat pits lie on the south and east sides of the pyramid; when investigated in modern times, two still contained wooden boats.

The substructure seems to have been constructed in three stages. First, a rock-cut descending passage was built, leading to what was to have been the first of a series of chambers deep under the centre of the pyramid. This series of chambers seems to have been abandoned when it was decided to include a stone sarcophagus in the burial, the passages being too low and narrow to introduce such a piece. An ascending corridor was thus added, apparently cutting through extant masonry, giving access to the so-called 'Queen's Chamber'. This could have received the sarcophagus before its walls were built, but plans seem to have changed again. The chamber is interesting, in that here the roof, instead of being corbelled, is of a new pointed type, which subsequently became standard for such rooms.

Above: The Great Pyramid at Giza, built by Khufu and still the most massive free-standing monument in the world. The entrance lies close to the centre of the north face.

Right: The Grand Gallery of Khufu's Great Pyramid leads up towards the burial chamber.

Plug-blocks were to be slid down the ascending passage after the burial, and to store them a corbelled room had been begun beyond the entrance to the passage leading into the Queen's Chamber. A shaft was also built to allow workmen to exit down to the descending passage after releasing them. The corbelled room was then greatly extended to become the 'Grand Gallery', giving access to the final burial chamber – the 'King's Chamber' – approached via an antechamber protected by portcullis slabs. Above the King's Chamber a series of relieving chambers were built; both the King's and the Queen's chambers had narrow (20 centimetres square) channels angled upwards from their north and south walls, apparently aimed at the stars. The channels from the King's Chamber continue to the exterior of the pyramid, but those of the Queen's Chamber were each blocked by a slab of stone with copper attachments. In at least one case, the shaft continued beyond

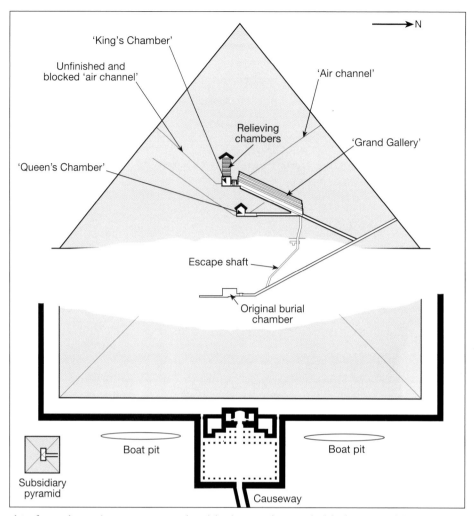

Right: Section of the Great Pyramid, and plan of the area in front of its east face.

Below: In the shadow of the Great Pyramid are the scanty remains of its subsidiary pyramid, whose entrance passage begins on the left.

this for a short distance to another blocking. This probably happened because the chamber was superseded by a new burial chamber, the position of the blocking corresponding to the level reached by the pyramid at the time the plan changed. The King's Chamber still contains the granite sarcophagus.

Principal Explorations

The pyramid was reopened by the Caliph Maamun during 813–33, when some elements of the original contents may still have been in place. The first proper survey was by Greaves in 1639. Investigations followed by Davison in 1765, Caviglia in 1817, Vyse and Perring in 1837 and a major survey by Petrie in 1880–82. The mortuary temple was excavated by Schiaparelli and Ballerini in 1903, Hassan in 1938–9 and Lauer in 1947. El-Mallakh found two pits containing dismantled boats in 1954. Hawass found the subsidiary pyramid in 1991.

DJEDEFRE'S PYRAMID

'Djedefre is a Shining Star'

Djedefre's Pyramid was built in a spectacular location, on a mountain top with views north into the delta, and south to Dahshur. The relatively modest size of the pyramid would thus have been more than offset by its visibility, lying some 20 metres higher than the Giza plateau. The structure is now very badly ruined, only the native rock core, plus a little masonry, being visible.

The remains of the mortuary temple are on the east side, and were partly constructed quickly in brick, suggesting the king's premature death. The remains of what seems to have been the subsidiary pyramid lie in the south-west corner of the enclosure, an unusual position otherwise found only at the Giza pyramid of Menkaure. The causeway leads, uniquely, from the north side of the complex to descend a 1.5-kilometre natural ridge. The valley building at the bottom has never been excavated, but must have lain close to the Third Dynasty El-Deir (Sanakhte's Tomb).

The substructure was built in a very deep T-shaped cutting, which placed the burial chamber far below the pyramid base. The corridors and chambers are, however, almost entirely destroyed. A fragment of what may have been an oval sarcophagus has been found.

Above: *The cutting for the entrance passage of Djedefre's Pyramid.*

Principal Explorations

The pyramid was surveyed by Perring in 1838–9 and Lepsius in 1842–3, and visited in 1881 by Petrie, who found the sarcophagus fragment. The mortuary temple was excavated by Chassinat in 1901–1903 and by Lacau around 1912. Valloggia began full clearance in 1994.

MODERN DESIGNATION: L.II.

LOCATION: Abu Rowash

DATE: *c.* 2547–2524 BC

OWNER: Djedefre

BASIS OF ATTRIBUTION: Numerous fragments of statues of the king have been found in the enclosure

DIMENSIONS: Base 106 x 106 metres

Left: *Plan of the pyramid complex of Djedefre.*

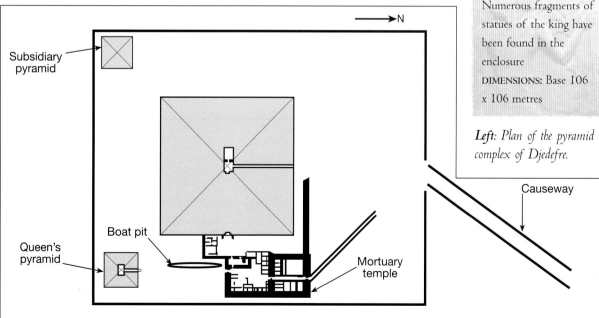

MODERN DESIGNATION:
L.XIII; Unfinished
Pyramid; Great Pit
LOCATION: Zawiyet el-
Aryan
DATE: c. 2516–2515 BC
OWNER: Seth?ka
BASIS OF ATTRIBUTION:
Quarry marks on blocks
give the king's name, the
first sign of which is
difficult to read (hence
the question mark in
the name). The king is
otherwise unknown, and
the pyramid was first
dated architecturally to
the Third Dynasty. It is
now agreed to be
Fourth Dynasty, and so
similar to Djedefre's
that the king is likely to
be his successor
DIMENSIONS: Base 200
x 200 metres

SETH?KA'S PYRAMID

Nothing of the superstructure of Seth?ka's monument survives; it may never have been begun. The T-shaped cutting for the substructure had been quarried and the pavement of the burial chamber – incorporating an oval sarcophagus – laid, before all work stopped.

Principal Explorations

Located by Lepsius in December 1842; substructure identified and cleared by Barsanti in 1904–11; a clearance for the filming of the movie *Land of the Pharaohs* was made in 1954. The monument is now within a military area and wholly inaccessible.

Above: Nothing of the superstructure of the Unfinished Pyramid at Zawiyet el-Aryan survives. Only the cutting for the substructure remains.

KHAEFRE'S PYRAMID

  'Great is Khaefre'

The second largest pyramid in Egypt, the angle of elevation on Khaefre's pyramid is, at 53 degrees, slightly greater than usual. Part of the casing survives near the summit.

The mortuary temple, causeway and valley building are all fairly well preserved, and mark a major step towards the standard pyramid complex. They are all built from particularly massive limestone masonry. The valley building was faced with ashlars of granite, its T-shaped hall containing a large number of fine statues, preserved through their placement in a pit in later times.

An almost completely destroyed subsidiary pyramid stood on the south side of the main pyramid, while the complex also incorporated the Great Sphinx and its associated temple. Although usually regarded as having been sculpted in the time of Khaefre, the Sphinx may have been carved during the Archaic Period. It is also possible that its head may have been completely recarved later, possibly during the Twelfth Dynasty reign of Amenemhat II, as a similar sphinx from that king's reign

Right: The Second Pyramid of Khaefre still has parts of the casing near its top.

MODERN DESIGNATION:
L.VIII; G II; Second
Pyramid
LOCATION: Giza
DATE: c. 2515–2493 BC
OWNER: Khaefre
BASIS OF ATTRIBUTION:
Numerous inscribed
statues in the pyramid's
temples
DIMENSIONS: Base 215
x 215 metres; height
143 metres

provides the best parallels for the details of the head of the Giza sphinx.

It may originally have been intended to build the pyramid somewhat north of its final location. This is suggested by its having essentially two substructures, the northernmost of the two with an entrance outside the north face and a burial chamber 30 metres north of the centre of the pyramid. Had the pyramid been further north (and of somewhat larger dimensions than finally employed), both would have been in a conventional position. The second set of galleries placed the final burial chamber roughly at ground level, marking the abandonment of deeply buried sepulchral chambers in pyramids. The new complex was linked to the old by a ramp, and protected by a portcullis slab. The sarcophagus was sunk in the floor of the burial chamber, with a cavity for the canopic containers in the floor to the south-east: the first surviving example of such a canopic installation within a pyramid.

Above: Near the foot of the causeway of the Second Pyramid crouches the Great Sphinx. It is possible that this dates from a slightly earlier period than the pyramid, and that its head may have been reworked during the Twelfth Dynasty.

Principal Explorations

The interior of the pyramid was opened by Belzoni in 1818, with the first major

Left: The Second Pyramid has a granite pillared hall that would once have been lined by statues of the king, Khaefre.

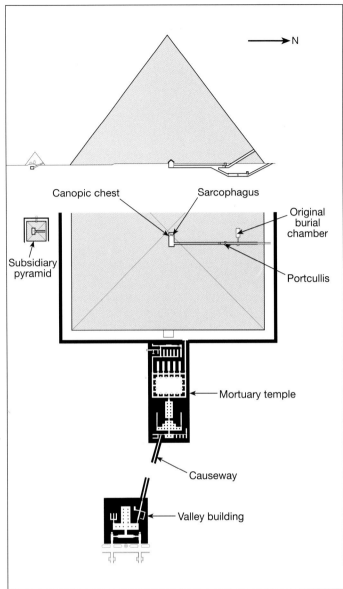

N

Canopic chest — Sarcophagus

Original burial chamber

Subsidiary pyramid

Portcullis

Mortuary temple

Causeway

Valley building

Above: The statues of Khaefre found in a pit in the temple hall of the valley building are now in the Cairo Museum.

Above right: Section and plan of the Second Pyramid.

examination of the whole monument undertaken by Vyse and Perring in 1837. The valley building was cleared by Mariette in 1853 and 1858, and surveyed by Petrie in 1881. The complex was fully cleared by Hölscher in 1909–10.

MENKAURE'S PYRAMID

 *'Menkaure is Divine'*

The Third Pyramid is very much smaller than the other two Giza pyramids; indeed, it seems originally to have been intended to be even smaller. It has lost all its limestone casing, but a large amount of a lower casing of granite is still in place.

The pyramid's temples show a further development over the temples of Khaefre, moving towards what was later to become the standard layout. The subsidiary pyramid (L.X/GIIIc) is near the south-west corner of the main monument, a position previously used by Djedefre, and later only by Userkaf.

The substructure of the main pyramid seems to have undergone at least two changes of plan. The initial small pyramid had a simple descending passage and burial chamber but, with the enlargement of the super-structure, a new entrance corridor was provided, including a small panelled chamber and three portcullises. Still later, a new burial chamber and a niched store-room were added at a lower level. The panelled basalt sarcophagus found in the final burial chamber was lost at sea en route to England in 1838. Menkaure's burial was renewed during the Twenty-fifth or Twenty-sixth Dynasty, when a new coffin was provided for his despoiled mummy. This coffin is in the British Museum, together with human remains that might be part of Menkaure's body, although carbon-14 dates suggest a much later derivation.

N

Original entrance

Subsidiary
pyramid (GIIIc)

Portcullises

GIIIb

GIIIa

Mortuary temple →

Causeway →

Valley building →

MODERN DESIGNATION
L.IX; G III; Third
Pyramid
LOCATION: Giza
DATE: *c.* 2493–2475 BC
OWNER: Menkaure
BASIS OF ATTRIBUTION
Inscription upon
pyramid casing and
many inscribed statues
and fragments in the
complex
DIMENSIONS: Base 103
x 103 metres; height 65
metres

Left: *Section and plan
of the Third Pyramid
complex.*

Below: *The Third Pyramid
still preserves substantial
remains of the mortuary
temple, from which the line
of the causeway can be
traced down to the valley
building, now buried
beneath the sand at the
bottom right of the picture.*

Principal Explorations

Many early European and Arab travellers mention the pyramid; masonry was removed in 1196 and 1827. Caviglia attempted to tunnel into the structure in 1836, and it was finally entered by Vyse and Perring in 1837; the pyramid's temples were excavated by Reisner during 1906–24.

MODERN DESIGNATION:
L.XLIII; D 66;
Mastabat Faraun
LOCATION: Saqqara-
South
DATE: c. 2475–2471 BC
OWNER: Shepseskaf
BASIS OF ATTRIBUTION:
Inscribed fragment
from mortuary temple
DIMENSIONS: Base 100
x 74 metres; height 18
metres

Above: The Mastabat Faraun of Shepseskaf at South Saqqara.

Below: Plan of the Mastabat Faraun.

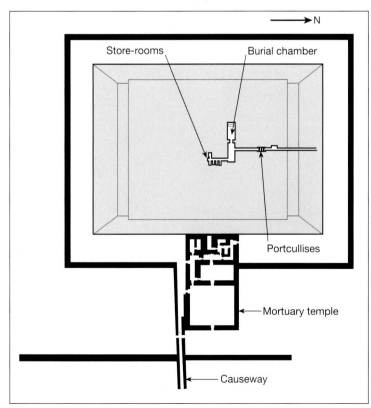

SHEPSESKAF'S TOMB

 *'Shepseskaf is Pure'*

Alone among the kings of the Old Kingdom whose monuments can be traced with certainty, Shepseskaf, last king of the Fourth Dynasty, did not begin a pyramid. Instead, he built a gigantic mastaba tomb, with raised end-pieces reminiscent of those found on the lids of many sarcophagi. This would seem to be a manifestation of the '*pr-nw*' shrine, a shape that is symbolic of Lower Egypt. The meaning of this change is unclear, although the abandonment of the solar symbol represented by the pyramid may be linked to the fact that the king's own name did not, unlike those of his immediate predecessors, contain the name of the sun-god, Re.

A conventional mortuary temple and causeway were built on the east side, but the valley building has never been explored. Likewise, nothing is known of any subsidiary tomb.

The substructure is similar to that of Menkaure's pyramid, but arranged more regularly, with the burial chamber west of an antechamber, and a room with store-niches to the south-east. The sarcophagus was smashed in antiquity.

Principal Explorations

The tomb was first entered by Mariette in the 1860s or 1870s; full clearance was carried out by Jéquier in 1924–5.

The Fifth Dynasty

Little is known of the transition between the Fourth and Fifth Dynasties, although it appears that a woman, Khentkaues I (see page 123), acted as regent at some point during the period. During the new dynasty, the principal royal necropolis was Abusir, some 11 kilometres south of Giza, although a number of kings were interred at Saqqara. The size and constructional quality of these pyramids falls well short of Fourth Dynasty norms, but in contrast, their temples are consistently larger and preserve very fine examples of relief decoration.

Above: North Saqqara: from the right are the pyramids of Userkaf, Djoser and Unas.

USERKAF'S PYRAMID

 *'Pure are the Places of Userkaf'*

Userkaf's pyramid, although relatively well built, has lost its casing, and is in fairly poor condition. Uniquely for its period, the majority of its mortuary temple is on the south side, probably as a result of the topography directly to the east not being conducive to pyramid building. The subsidiary pyramid is to the south-west, but the majority of the causeway and the valley building have not been discovered.

The substructure generally follows Shepseskaf's pattern, except that the storeroom is placed halfway along the entrance corridor and lacks niches. A broken sarcophagus was found in the burial chamber.

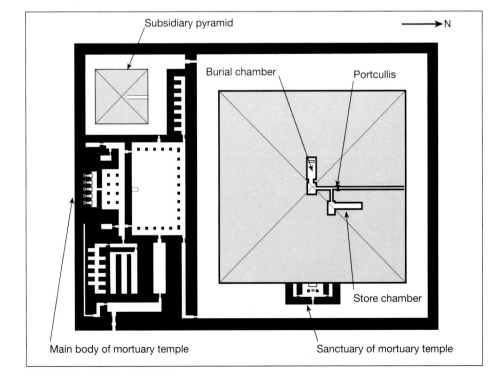

Subsidiary pyramid — Burial chamber — Portcullis — N — Store chamber — Main body of mortuary temple — Sanctuary of mortuary temple

Left: Plan of the pyramid complex of Userkaf.

MODERN DESIGNATION: L.XXXI; Haram el-Mekarbesh (Scratched Pyramid)
LOCATION: Saqqara
DATE: c 2471–2464 BC
OWNER: Userkaf
BASIS OF ATTRIBUTION: Many inscribed items in the pyramid complex
DIMENSIONS: Base 73 x 73 metres; height 49 metres

Above: The pyramid of Userkaf seen from the north-east.

Principal Explorations

The pyramid was opened by Marucchi (of whom very little is known) in 1831–2, and subsequently by Perring in July 1839, via a robber's tunnel. The mortuary temple was excavated by Firth in 1928–9; work was continued between 1948 and 1955 by Lauer, who returned for further work with Labrousse in 1976–8. Finally, El-Khouli worked on the site in 1982–5.

SAHURE'S PYRAMID

  *'The Ba of Sahure Appears'*

Right: Looking up the causeway of Sahure's pyramid.

The pyramid is in poor condition, and the area over the entrance corridor has collapsed. The mortuary temple is fairly well preserved, and follows a plan that

MODERN DESIGNATION: L.XVIII

LOCATION: Abusir

DATE: *c.* 2464–2452 BC

OWNER: Sahure

BASIS OF ATTRIBUTION: Numerous inscribed elements from the pyramid complex

DIMENSIONS: Base 79 x 79 metres; height 47 metres

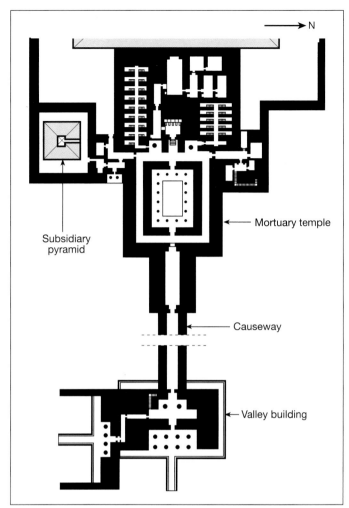

Subsidiary pyramid

Mortuary temple

Causeway

Valley building

essentially sets the standard for the remainder of the Old Kingdom. The causeway is also well pre-served, although the valley building is in poor shape, and partly below the modern water table. The sub-sidiary pyramid was placed just south of the mortuary temple, in what was hence-forth the standard location.

The interior of the pyramid was wrecked in the Middle Ages by stone robbers, leaving a partly collapsed, irregu-lar set of cavities,

Above: Many fragments of the decoration of the mor-tuary temple of Sahure's Pyramid survive. This one of Sahure being suckled by the goddess Nekhbet is in the Cairo Museum; their eyes were once inlaid with metal and stone.

Left: Plan of the mortuary temple and valley building of Sahure.

with just a single fragment of basalt representing the sarcophagus. The burial chamber lay in the centre of the pyramid; on the basis of later monuments, it is likely that an antechamber lay directly east of it, from which a horizontal passage led at a modestly oblique angle towards the centre of the north face. The actual entrance was a short sloping passage, with a portcullis at its inner end.

Principal Explorations
Investigated and entered by Perring in 1839, and again by de Morgan in the 1890s; excavated by Borchardt in 1902–1908.

NEFERIRKARE'S PYRAMID
 *'The Ba of Neferirkare'*

The pyramid core was built in stepped form, and it is possible that it was never cased as a true pyramid. Only the inner part of the mortuary temple was completed in stone, the remainder having been completed in brick and wood after Neferirkare's death. An important set of papyri relating to the running of the tem-ple were found in the mortuary temple. The causeway was later diverted to serve the pyramid of Niuserre, the valley building also being taken over by that king.

MODERN DESIGNATION: L.XXI; Great Pyramid (of Abusir)
LOCATION: Abusir
DATE: *c.* 2452–2442 BC
OWNER: Neferirkare Kakai
BASIS OF ATTRIBUTION: Inscribed material from complex
DIMENSIONS: Base 105 x 105 metres; height 72 metres

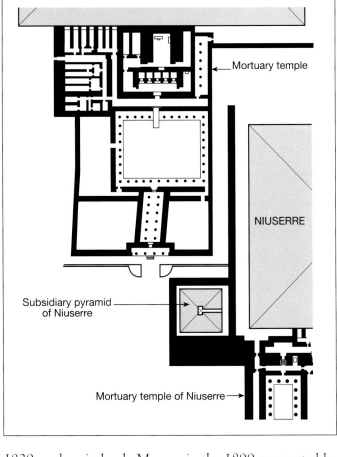

Above: The pyramid of Neferirkare, which may never have been cased.

Right: Plan of the mortuary temple of Neferirkare, where an important set of papyri on the running of the temple were found.

The interior of the pyramid was another victim of stone robbers, and little more than the general layout can be discerned.

Principal Explorations

Investigated and entered by Perring in 1839, and again by de Morgan in the 1890s; excavated by Borchardt in 1902–1908.

NEFEREFRE'S PYRAMID

 *'The Bas of Neferefre are Divine'*

Right: The monument of Neferefre rises only a few courses above the surrounding desert, and is dwarfed by the adjacent pyramid of Neferirkare.

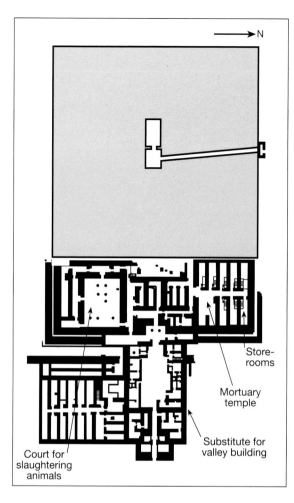

Left: Plan of the pyramid complex of Neferefre.

Court for slaughtering animals

Substitute for valley building

Mortuary temple

Store-rooms

Although intended to follow the pattern of earlier pyramids, this monument had only risen a few courses when the king died. Accordingly, it was finished off by filling the interior with gravel, thus turning it into a mastaba of uniquely square plan. Since the causeway and valley building were barely begun, the mortuary temple, largely built in brick, was enlarged to incorporate elements usually found in the valley building. The structure is well preserved, and revealed many items, including a wooden boat, statuary and administrative papyri.

The substructure followed the usual pattern for the period, but suffered severely from stone robbery owing to its coverage by little more than rubble.

MODERN DESIGNATION: L.XXVI; Unfinished Pyramid
LOCATION: Abusir
DATE: *c.* 2435–2432 BC
OWNER: Neferefre
BASIS OF ATTRIBUTION: Inscribed and written material from complex
DIMENSIONS: Base 65 x 65 metres

Nevertheless, along with fragments of the sarcophagus parts of the royal mummy were found, including a hand, part of the skull and other fragments. These mummified parts proved to be those of a young man.

Principal Explorations
Summarily examined by Borchardt in 1906, who believed that there was nothing to be found. Excavated by Verner and Bartá from 1985 onwards, whose important discoveries contradicted their predecessor's conclusions.

SHEPSEKARE'S PYRAMID (?)
The outline of a barely begun pyramid lies under the sand to the north of the other Abusir pyramids. The T-shaped cut for the substructure is visible, but little else; it seems that only one or two months' work was ever carried out.

MODERN DESIGNATION: None
LOCATION: Abusir
DATE: *c.* 2442–2435 BC
OWNER: Shepseskare?
BASIS OF ATTRIBUTION: Position and lack of any other likely monument for king
DIMENSIONS: Uncertain

Principal Explorations
Located by Verner in 1980.

Above: Neferefre's brick mortuary temple is well preserved; the outer part has been reburied after excavations.

MODERN DESIGNATION:
L.XX
LOCATION: Abusir
DATE: c. 2432–2421 BC
OWNER: Niuserre
BASIS OF ATTRIBUTION:
Inscribed material from
complex
DIMENSIONS: Base 79 x
79 metres; height 52
metres

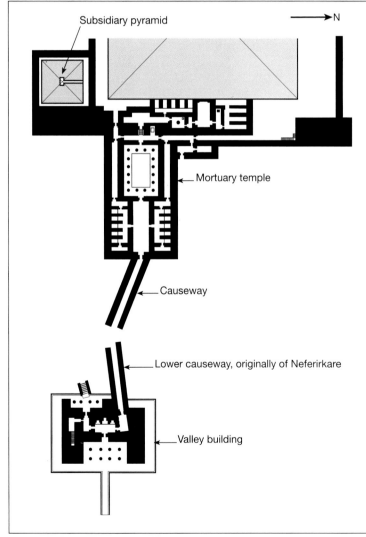

Above: The pyramid complex of Niuserre, seen from the pyramid's causeway.

Left: Plan of the mortuary temple of Niuserre, and the valley building he usurped from Neferirkare.

NIUSERRE'S PYRAMID

'*The Places of Niuserre are Established*'
The pyramid is of the usual construction for its period. The lower causeway and valley building of Neferirkare's pyramid were reused, the outer parts of Niuserre's mortuary temple being placed further south than usual to facilitate the construction of the new upper (joining) section of the causeway.

Here, too, the substructure was badly damaged by stone robbers who sought large fine limestone blocks for building the monuments of Cairo.

Principal Explorations
Examined and entered by Perring in 1839, and again by De Morgan in the 1890s; excavated by Borchardt in 1902–1908.

MENKAUHOR'S PYRAMID

'Divine are the Places of Menkauhor'
For plan, see page 74.

Nothing of this pyramid is now visible, although its general outline has been traced by modern investigators. It is possible that the causeway or valley building – traces of which could be seen in the 1840s – may have been reused for the complex of Teti, which lies to the west-south-west and has the outer parts of its mortuary temple arranged in such a way as to suggest orientation towards the earlier structure. What little is known of its sub-structure suggests the typical early Fifth Dynasty arrangement of an oblique entrance passage, an antechamber and a burial chamber. The monument has also been ascribed to the Tenth Dynasty king Merykare (see page 79), but the size and design are more consistent with a Fifth Dynasty date.

Most of the complex area was heavily built upon during the Graeco-Roman period, partly to provide the entrance way to the avenue of the Serapeum, the cemetery of the sacred bulls, which led west from this part of Saqqara, and to the cat and dog cemeteries that lay at the edge of the escarpment.

Principal Explorations
Noted by Lepsius in 1843 and superficially examined by Firth in 1930.

MODERN DESIGNATION: L.XXIX; Destroyed Pyramid
LOCATION: Saqqara
DATE: *c.* 2421–2413 BC
OWNER: Menkauhor
BASIS OF ATTRIBUTION: Design of interior, presence of monuments bearing Menkauhor's name in general area; its location near the edge of the escarpment mirrors that of the pyramid of Menkauhor's successor, Isesi
DIMENSIONS: Base *c.* 65–70 metres square

Above: King Menkauhor, as shown in an Eighteenth Dynasty relief from the tomb of Amenemonet at Saqqara.

Below: The pyramid of Isesi, seen from its mortuary temple.

ISESI'S PYRAMID

'Perfect is Isesi'

This pyramid follows the usual constructional style of the period. The mortuary temple is somewhat larger than those at Abusir, with a large 'pylon' on either side of the entrance. The causeway ascends the edge of the escarpment at a fairly steep angle; the valley building has not been found.

MODERN DESIGNATION:
L.XXXXVII; Haram
el-Shawwaf (Pyramid
of the Sentinel)
LOCATION: Saqqara-
South
DATE: c. 2413–2385 BC
OWNER: Djedkare Isesi
BASIS OF ATTRIBUTION:
Inscribed material from
complex
DIMENSIONS: Base 79 x
79 metres; reconstruct-
ed height 53 metres

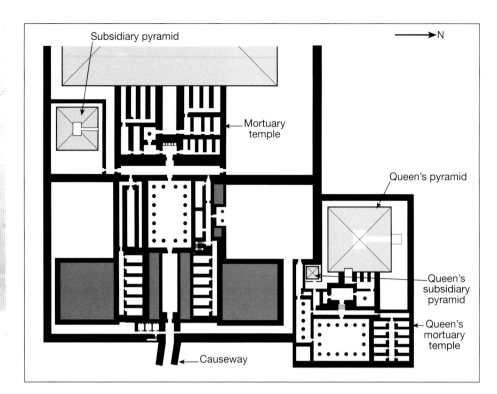

*Right: Plan of the
mortuary temple of
Isesi and the pyramid
complex of his wife.*

The substructure introduces a new standard plan: the antechamber now has doors in both west and east walls, the latter giving access to a store-room, probably with three niches. The burial chamber had its canopic chest sunk in the floor, south-east of the foot of the sarcophagus, which was broken by robbers; among the sarcophagus's fragments were the remains of Isesi's mummy, now in Cairo Museum.

Principal Explorations

Examined by Perring in 1839 and Lepsius in 1843, and entered by Maspero in 1880. Cleared by Varille and Abdelsalam Hussein in 1945, work being continued by Fakhry. New investigations began under Mathieu in April 2001.

UNAS' PYRAMID

 *'Perfect are the Places of Unas'*

MODERN DESIGNATION:
L.XXXV
LOCATION: Saqqara
DATE: c. 2385–2355 BC
OWNER: Unas
BASIS OF ATTRIBUTION:
Inscriptions inside and
outside the pyramid
DIMENSIONS:
Base 58 x 58 metres;
reconstructed height 43
metres

The funerary complex of Unas was built across the site of the Second Dynasty tomb of Hotepsekhemwy, the superstructure of which was demolished to make way for it. This enabled the complex to sit on the 'podium' created for the Archaic tomb.

Externally, the pyramid of Unas closely follows Fifth Dynasty patterns. Similarly, the mortuary temple is like that of Isesi, although lacking the latter's 'pylons'. Its causeway, of very considerable length owing to the complex's remote location, is perhaps the best preserved of its kind, with elements of the wall decoration in situ. The valley building is also in a fairly good state, and is interesting in that part of it was later used as the burial place of an early First Intermediate Period prince, Ptahshepses, in a borrowed Fourth Dynasty sarcophagus.

Internally, Unas' monument is essentially identical in design with that of Djedkare Isesi, but with some important additions: first, a chapel was built over the

Above: *The pyramid complex of Unas.*

Right: *Plan of Unas' complex.*

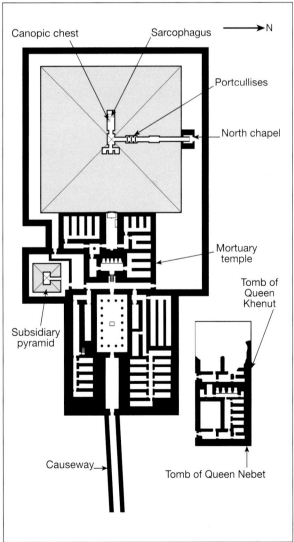

entrance to the substructure; second, the pyramid has the first royal substructure to be decorated since the time of Djoser. The west end of the burial chamber has a delicate panelled design, while the ceiling is adorned with five-pointed stars. Most importantly, the rest of the burial chamber, the antechamber and part of the approach corridor are covered with columns of hieroglyphs – the so-called Pyramid Texts, a compilation of religious spells (see page 14) that from this time became the standard decorative scheme for kingly pyramids until the end of the Old Kingdom. Interestingly, decoration also appears at this time in some private burial chambers, which hitherto had likewise been devoid of adornment.

Fragments of Unas' skull and left arm found in the burial chamber are now in Cairo Museum.

Principal Explorations

First entered by Maspero on 28 February 1881; the complex was cleared by Barsanti between 1899 and 1901, by Firth in 1929–30, by Hassan and Goneim in 1937–8, and by Saad and Hussein between 1939 and 1941. Hussein continued alone in 1941–3 and 1949; further work was done by Lauer and Leclant in 1974–5, Moussa in 1971 and Labrousse in 1990.

MODERN DESIGNATION:
L.XXX

LOCATION: Saqqara

DATE: *c.* 2355–2343 BC

OWNER: Teti

BASIS OF ATTRIBUTION: Inscriptions throughout the complex

DIMENSIONS: Base 79 x 79 metres; reconstructed height 52 metres

The Sixth Dynasty
TETI'S PYRAMID

'The Places of Teti Endure'

Above: The west end of the gable-roofed burial chamber of Teti, showing the incised panelling, the Pyramid Texts and the star-spangled ceiling.

The whole pyramid complex of Teti is very similar to that of Unas. In contrast to the latter, however, it lies close to the edge of the Saqqara escarpment, and it is possible that it reused the lower part of the causeway of the probable pyramid of Menkauhor, just to the east. Supporting this theory is the unusual offset entrance to Teti's mortuary temple.

The substructure of Teti's pyramid is identical with that of Unas, the only substantive difference being that the sarcophagus is internally decorated with the king's name and titles. Unlike the almost pristine interior of Unas' pyramid, that of Teti's was badly damaged by stone robbers – although not as severely as the Abusir pyramids. A shoulder and arm from the king's mummy were found in the chamber when it was opened.

Below: The area of the pyramid of Teti at Saqqara, showing the probable pyramid of Menkauhor, those of Teti's wives and some of the major private tombs of the period.

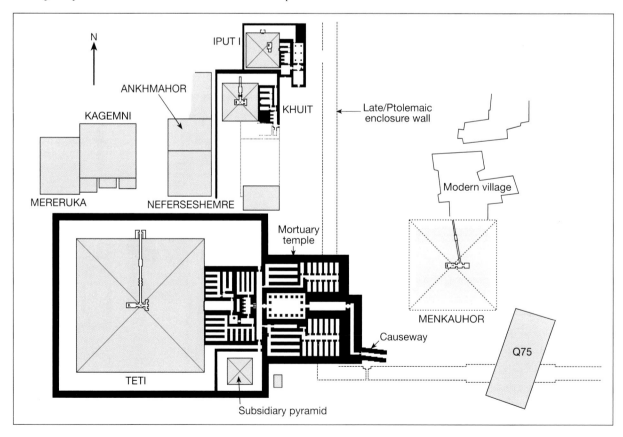

Principal Explorations

The substructure was first opened by Maspero on 29 May 1881; the mortuary temple was investigated by Quibell in 1907 and by Lauer and Leclant in 1965. The area north of the pyramid was cleared by Firth in 1921–2, the interior by Lauer and Sainte Fare Garnot in 1951–6.

PEPY I'S PYRAMID

'The Perfection of Meryre is Established'

The now very badly ruined pyramid complex of Pepy I followed usual Sixth Dynasty patterns. The interior also suffered at the hands of robbers, attempts even being made to break up the sarcophagus, which had been inscribed along the upper edge of its cof-fer. Besides the canopic chest, sunk as usual in the floor of the chamber, fragments of the canopic jars have come to light, together with the solidified contents of two of them. In addition, a hand and some bandages of the royal mummy survived.

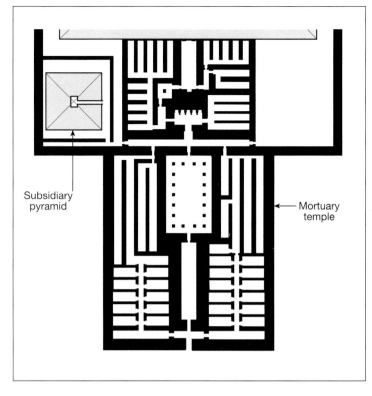

Subsidiary pyramid

Mortuary temple

Above: Plan of the mortuary temple of Pepy I.

Principal Explorations

The tomb was first entered by a local villager – via a hole in the roof of the exposed burial chamber – closely followed by Shahin in May 1880. Copies of the texts within were made soon afterwards by Emile Brugsch and also, surreptitiously, by Petrie, who found a mummified hand in the debris. This work revealed for the first time that some pyramids were decorated, as against the contemporary view that they were 'mute'. Petrie's 'pirate' copies appeared in a British periodical in April 1881, beating the official account of Heinrich Brugsch – who had copied the texts on 11 February 1881 – to the press by a month. The wrecked interior of the pyramid was cleared and restored by Lauer and Leclant in 1966–73, and the exterior parts excavated by Labrousse in 1979, 1987–8 and 1993–7.

Left: The pitiful remains of the pyramid of Pepy I, distinguishable only by the white limestone chips generated by its demolition.

MODERN DESIGNATION: L.XXXVI

LOCATION: Saqqara-South

DATE: *c.* 2343–2297 BC

OWNER: Nefersahor/Meryre Pepy I

BASIS OF ATTRIBUTION: Inscriptions throughout complex

DIMENSIONS: Base 79 x 79 metres; reconstructed height 52 metres

NEMTYEMSAF I'S PYRAMID

 *'The Perfection of Merenre Appears'*

MODERN DESIGNATION:
L.XXXIX

LOCATION: Saqqara-
South

DATE: *c.* 2297–2290 BC

OWNER: Merenre
Nemtyemsaf I

BASIS OF ATTRIBUTION:
Inscriptions within
pyramid

DIMENSIONS: Base 79 x
79 metres; reconstruct-
ed height 52 metres

This monument is nearly as badly destroyed as that of Nemtyemsaf's predecessor, both inside and out. The sarcophagus – which, like the canopic chest, survived large-ly undamaged and was made of greywacke – was decorated externally with the royal names and titles, with the innovation that the edge of the lid also bore texts. A mummy was found within the sarcophagus, but it remains a matter of debate whether it belonged to the king or, as is perhaps more likely, a later intrusive burial.

Principal Explorations

Opened by Shahin in December 1880, it was examined on 4 January 1881 by the Brugsch brothers, who removed the mummy found there. This was first carried to the local railway station in a wooden box. Unfortunately, the train had to terminate short of Cairo, meaning that the Germans had to walk the last few kilometres. The box proving too heavy, the mummy was then carried without covering – until it broke in half! One brother carrying each part, they eventually caught a cab to the museum, paying customs duty on their burden as 'pickled fish' when they crossed into the city via the Qasr el-Nil bridge.

While the temples of the pyramid remain unexcavated, the interior of the pyramid was cleared and restored by Lauer in 1971–3.

Right: Nemtyemsaf I's pyramid, seen from the west, is another pyramid in a rather poor state.

PEPY II'S PYRAMID

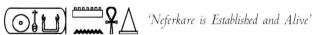 *'Neferkare is Established and Alive'*

MODERN DESIGNATION
L.XLI

LOCATION: Saqqara-
South

DATE: *c.* 2290–2196
BC

OWNER: Neferkare Pepy
II

BASIS OF ATTRIBUTION:
Inscriptions throughout
complex

DIMENSIONS: Base 79 x
79 metres; reconstruct-
ed height 53 metres

Pepy II's pyramid is much better preserved than those of his immediate predecessors, and seems to have been built with rather more care. When it was at least partly built, a masonry 'girdle' 6.5 metres thick was added around the lower part of the structure; this may have been because the structure was feared to be unstable, perhaps after an earthquake. The construction of this feature meant that

Above: Pepy II's monument is in rather better condition than Nemtyemsaf's or Pepy I's.

Right: Plan of the complex of Pepy II, including the pyramids of some of his wives.

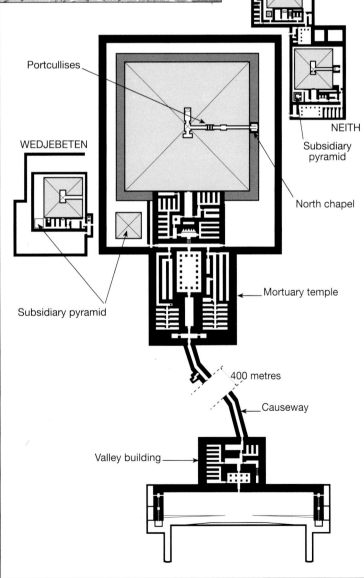

the north chapel had to be dismantled and rebuilt further out.

The complex itself represents the Old Kingdom royal tomb at its most developed, with all aspects preserved to some extent. Parts of the mortuary temple have been restored with elements of the decoration in place.

The substructure once again follows contemporary norms, and is not as badly damaged by stone robbers as most of the other pyramids of the period. In contrast to that of Nemtyemtsaf I, the (broken) box of the canopic chest was of alabaster, although the lid was still of hardstone. The sarcophagus has only one row of texts on its exterior.

Principal Explorations

The pyramid was first opened by Shahin for Maspero in February–April 1881; the complex was fully excavated by Jéquier in 1932–5.

THE FIRST INTERMEDIATE PERIOD

Following the very long reign of Pepy II, there seems to have been a rapid decline in central power, manifested in a succession of brief reigns, known as the Seventh/Eighth Dynasty. This dynasty continued to reign at Memphis, but the power of the southern provincial governers grew rapidly. Ultimately, the country split with the Ninth/Tenth Dynasty ruling from Herakleopolis and the Eleventh at Thebes. A civil war presaged forcible reunification under the southern Eleventh Dynasty.

The Seventh/Eighth Dynasty

IBI'S PYRAMID

MODERN DESIGNATION:
L.XL
LOCATION: Saqqara-South
DATE: *c.* 2185 BC
OWNER: Qakare Ibi
BASIS OF ATTRIBUTION:
Inscriptions within pyramid
DIMENSIONS: Base 32 x 32 metres

This monument reflects the collapse of royal power, the unfinished pyramid itself being no larger than a queen's example of the preceding era. Only a few parts of the superstructure survive, along with traces of a small mud-brick mortuary temple. The substructure was reduced to two rooms, albeit still decorated with the Pyramid Texts.

Principal Explorations
Excavated by Jéquier in 1929–31.

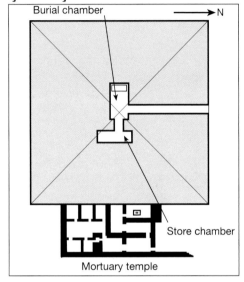

Above right: Plan of Ibi's Pyramid, which is no larger than that of an Old Kingdom queen.

Right: The scant ruins of the pyramid of Ibi.

The Ninth/Tenth Dynasty

These dynasties are little known, except that they ruled from Herakleopolis, near the mouth of the Fayoum depression. Even the names of the kings of these dynasties are uncertain, as are their burial places. One tomb is known of, thanks to written sources, and another is dated to the period on archaeological grounds.

KHUI'S PYRAMID (?)

This mysterious brick structure is of considerable size, bigger than all brick pyramids except that at Abu Rowash. Its dating is very uncertain, Khui being otherwise unknown. Of the structure's intended form, only the square plan suggests a pyramid. The substructure is unique, apparently entered via a horizontal vaulted passage in the middle of the north side.

Beyond this vaulted passage, a vestibule has a stairway running upwards to the left and a passage to the right; their destination has been destroyed, along with most of the interior of the superstructure. A passage descends from the end of the vestibule, its roof supported by a series of brick arches until it ends abruptly in a small stone-lined burial chamber. The burial chamber's floor is, very oddly, at the same angle as the passage, with its ceiling at a slightly shallower angle. This would suggest a hurried change of plan – presumably the intended burial chamber would have been further south.

Principal Explorations

Kamal first excavated the structure in 1911; further work was done by Weill in 1946–8.

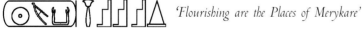

Above: Section of the mysterious monument of Dara.

MERYKARE'S PYRAMID

'Flourishing are the Places of Merykare'

Our knowledge of the very existence of this monument derives solely from the texts on the stelae of a number of mortuary priests of the monument. Several of the texts claim that the pyramid shared its priesthood with that of the pyramid of Teti. It is generally assumed that the two pyramids of Teti and Merykare lay near one another, although an earlier mortuary priest, Shery, was buried at Saqqara, but had cult responsibilities for Peribsen, buried over 300 kilometres away at Abydos. Merykare's pyramid has frequently been identified with L.XXIX, directly east of Teti's, but the apparent plan of that seems far more appropriate for the Fifth Dynasty's Menkauhor (see above, page 71). It is conceivable that Merykare might have usurped Menkauhor's monument, but without its proper excavation conclusions are impossible.

MODERN DESIGNATION: Dara M

LOCATION: Dara (Arab el-Amaiem; Beni Qurra)

DATE: *c.* 22nd/21st century BC

OWNER: Khui?

BASIS OF ATTRIBUTION: Name of king found in a nearby tomb; pottery from the site is of First Intermediate Period type

DIMENSIONS: Base 130 x 130 metres

MODERN DESIGNATION: ?

LOCATION: Saqqara (?)

DATE: *c.*2042 BC

OWNER: Merykare

BASIS OF ATTRIBUTION: Inscriptions on stelae of mortuary priests (see main text)

DIMENSIONS: Not known

THE EVOLUTION OF THE PYRAMID: THE MIDDLE KINGDOM

Below: Apart from the pyramid itself, only a few stone fragments survive from Amenemhat III's complex at Hawara.

The Eleventh Dynasty

The first kings of the Eleventh Dynasty ruled southern Egypt only. They ruled from their capital of Thebes, and this is where they were buried. Later monarchs reunified the nation, but continued to be buried in the cemeteries that lay across the river from the Theban temples.

CHRONOLOGY OF THE MIDDLE KINGDOM

MIDDLE KINGDOM
DYNASTY XIa (2160–2066) DYNASTY XIb (2080–1994) DYNASTY XII (1994–1781)

Inyotef I Inyotef II Inyotef III Montjuhotpe II Montjuhotpe III Amenemhat I Senwosret I Amenemhat II Senwosret II Senwosret III Amenemhat III Amenemhat IV Sobkne

HEAD OF
MONTJUHOTPE II

SPHINX OF
AMENEMHAT II

BUST OF
AMENEMHAT III

FACE OF
SENWOSRET III

INYOTEF I'S TOMB

The surviving portion of this tomb is a sunken courtyard, with a double colonnade across the rear, providing the façade for the royal offering place. A series of door-ways at the sides gives access to the tombs of members of the court. Such tombs are known as 'saffs', from the Arabic for 'row'. Below the central royal chapel descend shafts lead to roughly hewn burial chambers.

Later documents refer to at least one of these tombs as 'pyramid', but no trace of any such element has been identified.

MODERN DESIGNATION: Saff el-Dawaba
LOCATION: El-Tarif
DATE: *c.* 2140–2123 BC
OWNER: Horus Sehertawy Inyotef I
BASIS OF ATTRIBUTION: Design and location relative to tombs of Inyotef II and III
DIMENSIONS: Courtyard 65 x 300 metres

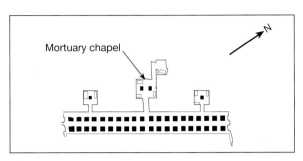

Principal Explorations

Surveyed in 1966 and excavated in 1970–74 by Arnold.

INYOTEF II'S TOMB

A very similar monument to the previous *saff*, but with many more chambers at the rear of the court. It is likely that the king's burial lay at the end of the sloping passage at the rear of the central chapel, but this remains unverified.

The tomb is described in Papyrus Abbott (British Museum). This papyrus is a record of an inspection of Theban royal tombs during the reign of Rameses IX, which describes the Saff el-Qisasiya as having 'the

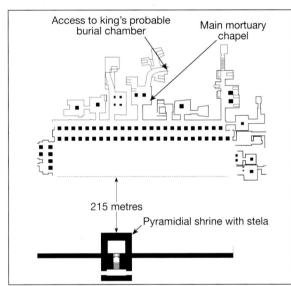

Left: The saff tombs of the Inyotefs. From the top: Saff el-Dawaba (Inyotef I), Saff el-Qisasiya (Inyotef II) and Saff el-Baqar (Inyotef III).

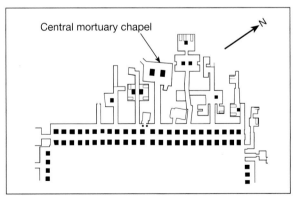

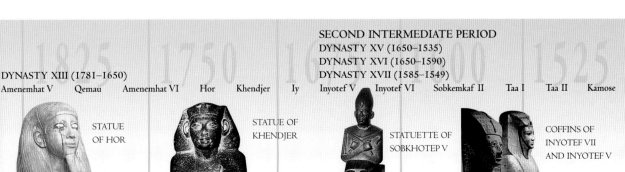

MODERN DESIGNATION:
Saff el-Qisasiya
LOCATION: El-Tarif
DATE: *c.* 2123–2074 BC
OWNER: Horus
Wahankh Inyotef II
BASIS OF ATTRIBUTION:
Various items of
inscribed material
DIMENSIONS: Courtyard
70 x 250+ metres

pyramid fallen down upon it, before which its stela stands; the figure of the king stands upon this stela, his dog between his feet'. The stela in question is now in the Cairo Museum; the brick chapel which held it, at the eastern end of the court – 250 metres from the main façade – was apparently of pyramidal form. The chapels and burial shafts of the tomb are of simple form at the rear of the courtyard. The whole tomb is today largely filled by modern houses.

Principal Explorations

The stela-chapel was located by Mariette in 1860, and the stela recovered by Maspero in 1884, further fragments being found by Daressy in 1889; Winlock obtained a number of stelae in 1913–14. The tomb was surveyed and excavated by Arnold in 1966 and 1970–74.

INYOTEF III'S TOMB

This tomb is essentially identical to the previous two monuments, but with a more elaborate stone-lined offering place. Sarcophagus fragments also suggest more sophisticated arrangements.

Principal Explorations

Surveyed in 1966 by Arnold, and excavated in 1971–4.

MODERN DESIGNATION: Saff el-Baqar
LOCATION: El-Tarif
DATE: *c.* 2074–2066 BC
OWNER: Horus Nakhtnebtepnefer Inyotef III
BASIS OF ATTRIBUTION: Typological
comparison with the tomb of Inyotef II
DIMENSIONS: Courtyard 75 metres wide,
length not known

MONTJUHOTPE II'S TEMPLE-TOMB

'Glorious are the places of Nebhepetre'

This sepulchre marks a complete departure from previous royal mortuary monuments. It comprises a terraced temple, with colonnades fronting each terrace, and peristyle and hypostyle elements further back. In the centre stood a square massif

Right: Aerial view of Deir el-Bahari. Montjuhotpe II's temple is on the left, that of the Eighteenth Dynasty Hatshepsut on the right. Thutmose III's temple was still buried under the debris between Montjuhotpe's and Hatshepsut's temples when this view was taken in the 1920s or 1930s.

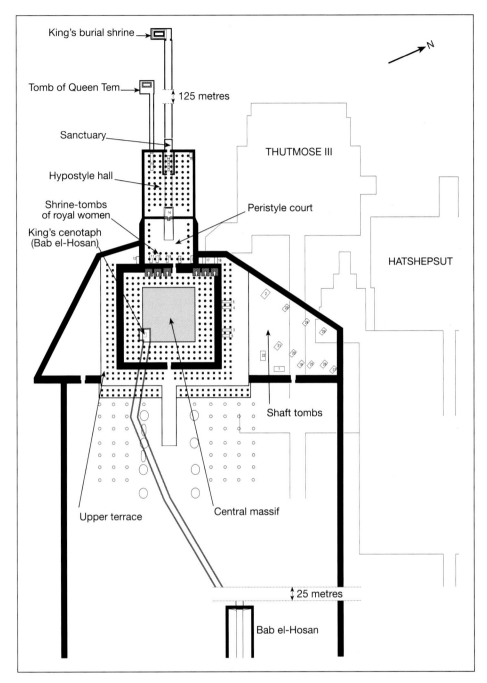

King's burial shrine

Tomb of Queen Tem

125 metres

Sanctuary

Hypostyle hall

Shrine-tombs
of royal women

King's cenotaph
(Bab el-Hosan)

THUTMOSE III

Peristyle court

HATSHEPSUT

Shaft tombs

Upper terrace

Central massif

25 metres

Bab el-Hosan

N

MODERN DESIGNATION:
Eleventh Dynasty
Temple; DBXI.14
LOCATION: Deir el-
Bahari
DATE: c. 2066–2014 BC
OWNER: Nebhepetre
Montjuhotpe II
BASIS OF ATTRIBUTION:
Numerous inscribed
elements from through-
out the complex
DIMENSIONS: Temple
axis 115 metres long

Left: *Plan of the temple
of Montjuhotpe II, showing
the location of the later
Eighteenth Dynasty temples
of Thutmose III and
Hatshepsut.*

of uncertain original form. The Abbott Papyrus (see page 106) calls the monument a pyramid, but the extant remains do not support such a reconstruction.

The temple was extensively decorated, with a sloping passageway in the rear
courtyard giving access to a long, sandstone-lined passage leading to the pointed-
roofed burial chamber (Tomb 14). Rather than a sarcophagus, the burial chamber
held an alabaster shrine. Most of the recovered fragments of the coffin, canopic jars
and mummy are in the British Museum. The monument also incorporated the burial places of members of the royal family and, in the forecourt, a dummy tomb for
the king (the Bab el-Hosan). The dummy tomb held a statue, an empty coffin and
some boats, and seems to have been used in Montjuhotpe II's jubilee ceremonies.

Principal Explorations
The rear part of the temple was discovered by Lord Dufferin in 1859–60 and the dummy tomb by Carter in 1901. The whole monument was then cleared by Naville in 1903–1906, and re-excavated by Winlock in 1920–24. Further work was led by Arnold in 1966–71.

Above: The entrance to the royal tomb of Montjuhotpe II in the rear courtyard of the temple.

THEBAN TOMB 281

The later of the two datings given in the information panel below is based on the advanced style of the material from the nearby tomb of Meketre (TT280), which, it has been argued, is inconsistent with the time of Montjuhotpe III. In addition, the unfinished state of the funerary complex of Amenemhat I at Lisht might suggest that this was an earlier tomb for the king at Thebes before he moved the royal capital and necropolis to the north, where subsequent royal tombs lay.

It appears that this structure was intended to be of the same kind as that of Montjuhotpe II. However, nothing was ever done other than filling and grading the platform for the temple itself and its causeway. A sloping passageway at the rear of the platform leads to a gable-roofed limestone burial chamber.

Below right: The temple platform begun by either Montjuhotpe III or Amenemhat I. The entrance to the tomb (TT281) is in the centre of the platform, towards the base of the cliff.

Principal Explorations
The burial chamber was discovered by Mond in 1903–1904, but the existence of the rest of the monument was noted only in 1914 by Winlock, who excavated the site in 1920–21.

MODERN DESIGNATION:
TT281
LOCATION: Sheikh Abd el-Qurna West
DATE: c. 2014–2001 or 1994–1964 BC
OWNER: Seankhkare Montjuhotpe III or Sehotepibre Amenemhat I (?)
BASIS OF ATTRIBUTION: Apparent similarity to tomb of Montjuhotpe II

The Twelfth Dynasty

AMENEMHAT I'S PYRAMID

'The Places of the Appearance of Amenemhat'

'Amenemhat is High and Beautiful'

Amenemhat I was responsible for moving the capital of Egypt back to the north, to a city known as Itjtawi. This seems to have lain near modern Lisht, where Amenemhat I built his tomb. As we have seen, it is possible that he may previously have begun a temple-tomb in the south, but at Lisht a broadly conventional pyramid complex was erected. The pyramid itself was of stone, albeit of poor quality, and incorporated numerous blocks from Old Kingdom pyramid complexes. This may simply reflect a desire for economy, but it is also possible that they were used physically to link Amenemhat with the great kings of the past. Certainly, his propaganda presented him as the founder of a new era, which would see Egypt restored to its past glories.

Little is known of the valley building and causeway, and the mortuary temple has been so thoroughly destroyed that virtually nothing is known of its plan. We can, however, assume that it remained unfinished. Surviving terracing shows that it had two levels, suggesting some affinity with Montjuhotpe II's sepulchre at Deir el-Bahari. There are indications that the design of the temple was altered in the course of construction. No trace of a subsidiary pyramid was found.

The substructure was entered from ground level on the north side, a granite-lined corridor leading to a square chamber under the

Right: Section and plan of Amenemhat I's pyramid complex.

MODERN DESIGNATION: L.LX; Northern Pyramid

LOCATION: Lisht

DATE: *c.* 1994–1964 BC

OWNER: Sehetepibre Amenemhat I

BASIS OF ATTRIBUTION: Inscribed material from complex

DIMENSIONS: Base 86 x 86 metres; reconstructed height 55 metres

N

Modern water table

372

North chapel

Upper terrace

470

Mortuary temple

463

954

956

Causeway

Possible queens' tombs

Lower terrace

Above: The pyramid of Amenemhat I at Lisht: it appears to lie on a higher level than the area of the destroyed mortuary temple, suggesting a possible arrangement akin to that found at Deir el-Bahari.

Right: A distant view of Senwosret I's innovative pyramid.

MODERN DESIGNATION: L.LXI; Southern Pyramid
LOCATION: Lisht
DATE: c. 1974–1929 BC
OWNER: Kheperkare Senwosret I
BASIS OF ATTRIBUTION: Inscribed material from complex
DIMENSIONS: Base 105 x 105 metres; height 61 metres

centre of the pyramid. From the centre of this room, a vertical shaft led down over 11 metres. Unfortunately, rising groundwater has inundated whatever lies below, and all attempts at pumping have failed. Likewise, no items of the king's funerary equipment have come to light.

Principal Explorations
Examined by Perring on 28 October 1839, Amenemhat I's tomb was first entered by Maspero in 1882. Excavations were then begun by Gautier and Jéquier in November 1894, followed by far more extensive ones by Lythgoe, Lansing and Mace collaboratively in 1906–1908, 1913–14 and 1920–22. The Egyptian Antiquities Organization did some clearance work at the valley building in the 1980s.

SENWOSRET I'S PYRAMID

 *'Senwosret Beholds the Two Lands'*

Amenemhat I's successor built his pyramid some 1,750 metres south of that of his father. Senwosret I's structure is innovative: it comprises a series of solidly built limestone retaining walls, with the intervening spaces filled with smaller blocks and rubble, embedded in mortar. The complex, of which the valley building remains undiscovered, closely follows late Old Kingdom norms in its design, including the last known example of a subsidiary pyramid. An unusual feature of the causeway was its partial lining with statues of the king. The outer part of the enclosure wall of the complex had finely carved bastions bearing the Horus-name of Senwosret I.

A chapel once stood over the pyramid entrance; as in Amenemhat I's pyramid, the burial chamber – some 24 metres below the pyramid base – is now under water, together with the lower end of the steeply sloped entrance corridor: the

shaft found in Amenemhat's pyramid is absent here. However, items of funerary equipment, displaced by robbers, were found above the water level, including the king's canopic jars. These are fairly unusual in having arms carved on their sides, although a private contemporary even had feet incorporated into his!

Principal Explorations

Examined by Perring on 28 October 1839, the pyramid was first entered by Maspero's workmen in 1882. Excavations were then carried out by Gautier and Jéquier in 1895–6, followed by far more extensive ones by Lythgoe and Lansing between 1908 and 1934. The latter excavations were undertaken under the auspices of the Metropolitan Museum of Art, New York, which resumed work under the direction of Arnold in 1984–7. These renewed excavations were undertaken so that Arnold could obtain the necessary information to proceed with the publication of the excavations of the pyramid complex.

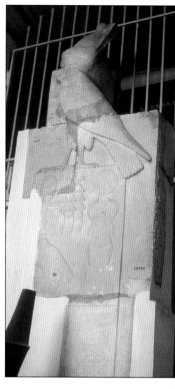

Above: One of the highly decorated panels from the enclosure wall of Senwosret I's Pyramid, bearing the king's Horus name – Ankhmesut – and praenomen, Kheperkare.

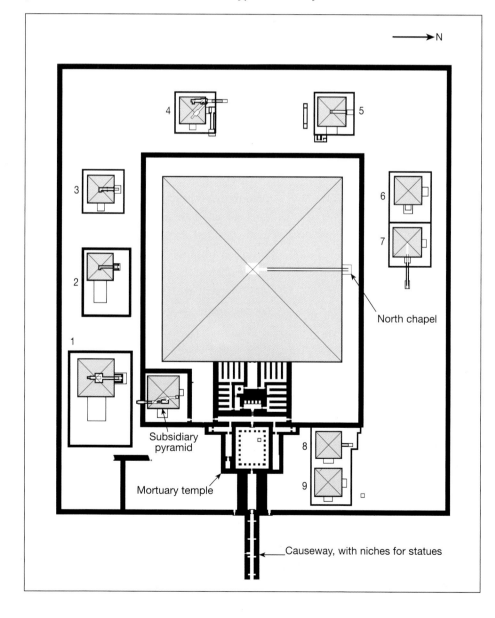

North chapel

Subsidiary pyramid

Mortuary temple

Causeway, with niches for statues

Left: Plan of the complex of Senwosret I, showing the nine pyramids belonging to members of the royal family.

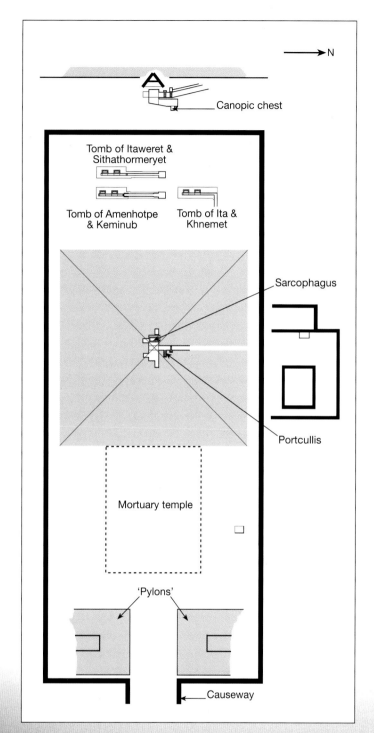

Canopic chest

Tomb of Itaweret &
Sithathormeryet

Tomb of Amenhotpe   Tomb of Ita &
& Keminub   Khnemet

Sarcophagus

Portcullis

Mortuary temple

'Pylons'

Causeway

AMENEMHAT II'S PYRAMID

'The Ba of Amenemhat'

The next king abandoned Lisht, and moved north to Dahshur. In contrast with Seneferu, who had built his pyramids some 2,000 metres out into the desert, Amenemhat II built his close to the edge of the desert, on the high ridge that lies only a short distance from the edge of cultivated land. It is situated directly south of an Old Kingdom cemetery, at least four of whose tombs were annexed into the north-west corner of the king's new enclosure. The pyramid itself has been so thoroughly destroyed – the remaining limestone chippings giving it its modern name of White Pyramid – that even the dimensions of its base cannot be determined. However, it seems to have used the same structural scheme as that of Senwosret I.

The rest of the complex is also in poor condition, but it can be seen to represent further divergence from the Old Kingdom prototype. First, the enclosure is extended both to the east and west. The area to the west holds a number of innovatively designed tombs, almost certainly belonging to members of the king's family, although later dates have been suggested. The area to the east accommodated the vanished

Left: *Plan of the White Pyramid complex, and a section of the pyramid's substructure.*

Below: *The utterly devastated White Pyramid of Amenemhat II is barely visible on the peak of the escarpment at Dahshur.*

mortuary temple, as well as two masonry masses, which may, like similar elements at the pyramid of Djedkare Isesi, represent some kind of pylon gateway.

The substructure is, at first sight, simple, but nevertheless has a number of interesting features. A corridor from the north leads, via two portcullises, to a flat-ceilinged burial chamber. Above this, however, is a set of gabled relieving beams. Inside the chamber the sarcophagus, made up from a series of quartzite slabs, was concealed under the floor. In some previous tombs, for example that of Khaefre, sarcophagus lids had been arranged to lie flush with the floor, but in the White Pyramid, filling and paving slabs had been laid over the sarcophagus cover. Hitherto, canopic chests had always lain south or south-east of the body. This one, however, lay in the floor of a short passage that led back under the pyramid entrance passage, ending up north-east of the body. These departures were clearly intended to enhance the protection given to the corpse, the next reign seeing yet further divergence from time-hallowed tradition.

Principal Explorations
De Morgan, between December 1894 and April 1895, carried out the only substantive work on this pyramid; he found the intact burials of four princesses in the western part of the enclosure; their jewellery is now in the Cairo Museum.

SENWOSRET II'S PYRAMID

'The Power of Senwosret'

Senwosret II constructed his tomb in the Fayoum region, an area remote from the usual royal necropolis in the Memphis area. This would seem to have been a

MODERN DESIGNATION: L.LI; White Pyramid
LOCATION: Dahshur
DATE: c. 1932–1896 BC
OWNER: Nubkaure Amenemhat II
BASIS OF ATTRIBUTION: Inscribed material from complex
DIMENSIONS: Base approx. 50 x 50 metres

MODERN DESIGNATION: L.LXVI
LOCATION: Lahun
DATE: c. 1900–1880 BC
OWNER: Kheperkhare Senwosret II
BASIS OF ATTRIBUTION: Inscribed material from complex
DIMENSIONS: Base 106 x 106 metres; reconstructed height 49 metres

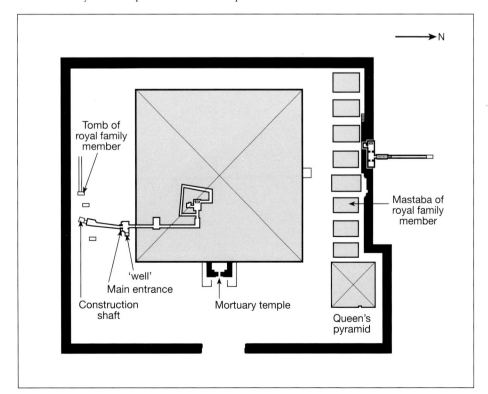

Left: The plan of the pyramid complex of Senwosret II at Lahun shows the radical change that the monument represented, with the burial places decisively shifted relative to their above-ground elements.

Above: Below Senwosret II's Pyramid at Lahun is a granite burial chamber containing a sarcophagus of unusual form.

Below: The core of Senwosret II's Lahun pyramid was also something different – a rock knoll surmounted by a framework of stone, filled with mud brick.

reflection of the interest shown in the Fayoum area by kings of his dynasty, a number of whom appear to have undertaken irrigation and land reclamation work there. It centres on a large lake, Birket Qarun, fed by the Bahr Yusef, an offshoot of the Nile which splits from it at Asyut.

The king's pyramid complex marks the most momentous set of changes in Egyptian funerary practice since the early Old Kingdom. While the basic concept of the pyramid, mortuary temple, causeway and valley building remained intact, the execution of the first element (the pyramid) incorporated fundamental rethinking. First, the pyramid itself was built of mud brick for the first time since the end of the Third Dynasty. As in the Brick Pyramid at Abu Rowash, a considerable portion of the core was composed of a native rock knoll. The brick was keyed into the rock by a set of radial stone walls built on top, very similar to the system employed at the pyramid of Senwosret I, except that the filling was now of brick. The usual Tura limestone was employed for the outermost casing.

Second, the entrance to the substructure was switched to the south side, with the burial chamber shifted away from the centre of the monument. At the same time, the entrance became a shaft and the corridors and chambers a tunnelled system – apparently necessitated by the use of the rock knoll for the pyramid core which prevented the usual 'cut and cover' approach. The inability to lower in heavy blocks from above resulted in the main entrance shaft being supplemented with a larger 'construction' shaft further south. This was concealed after use under the floor of a dummy tomb, reflecting the underlying motivation of security. The same imperative is also seen elsewhere in the complex. On the north side are eight mastabas, with their cores cut from the living rock like the main pyramid, and the queen's pyramid (page 132). However, none has its substructure below the pyramid, and the burial passages of the mastabas lie in front of the south face of the king's pyramid.

Senwosret II's substructure is

fairly simple, but has some curious features, including a deep shaft near the entrance leading down to the water table and a corridor that runs round three sides of the burial chamber. The chamber itself, gable-roofed and of granite, holds a sarcophagus with an irregular undersurface and a thick lip round the rim. Perhaps an early plan had called for the sarcophagus to be partly sunk in the burial chamber floor. When excavated, the room was found to contain an alabaster offering table, the gold cobra from the king's crown and a pair of leg bones, the last traces of the pharaoh himself.

Above: Among the contents of Senwosret II's Pyramid at Lahun was an alabaster offering table.

The rest of the complex has been badly depleted, although the settlement of Lahun that adjoined the valley building has preserved much information on the daily life of the Middle Kingdom. This includes documents as well as domestic items.

Principal Explorations

The site was examined by the French and Prussian expeditions of the 1820s and 1840s, as well as by Perring on 31 October 1839, but it was not until 1889–90 that excavations properly began, carried out by Petrie. He resumed work in 1913–14, completing his excavations in 1920–21. Further excavations have been carried out by Millet from 1989 onwards.

SENWOSRET III'S PYRAMID

 *'Pure is Senwosret'*

The next monarch forsook the Fayoum in favour of the ancient cemetery of Dahshur, building his tomb 1,500 metres north of that of Amenemhat II. Senwosret III's monument is, however, another innovative achievement, although not quite in the same way as that of Senwosret II. It continues the use of brick for the actual pyramid, but without the use of a rock knoll; today, the pyramid is in a poor state, having been badly mutilated by 19th-century excavators.

The pyramid complex underwent at least two phases of building. The first followed a design not dissimilar to that found at Lahun, with royal family tombs placed within the enclosure, north and south of the king's pyramid (see page 133). However, the final version produced a rectangular enclosure strikingly similar in appearance to that of Djoser of the Third Dynasty. Not only was the enclosure wall panelled, but the king's sarcophagus had a panelled motif applied to its lower part that seems to have been intended to replicate the actual pattern of bastions seen on Djoser's monument. In addition, the entrance to the enclosure was in the south-east corner, an arrangement not seen since the Third Dynasty. Finally, in two shafts at the northern end of the complex, in an area enclosed by the final enlargement, were two Third Dynasty alabaster sarcophagi, apparently not used for burials. They are identical with examples found under the Step Pyramid, and it

MODERN DESIGNATION: L.XLVII; North Brick Pyramid

LOCATION: Dahshur

DATE: *c.* 1900–1880 BC

OWNER: Khakaure Senwosret III

BASIS OF ATTRIBUTION: Inscribed material from complex

DIMENSIONS: Base 105 x 105 metres; reconstructed height 78 metres

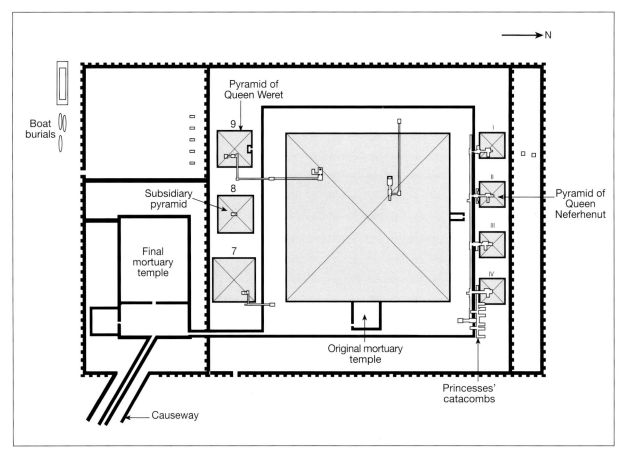

Boat burials

Pyramid of Queen Weret

9

Subsidiary pyramid

8

Final mortuary temple

7

Original mortuary temple

Pyramid of Queen Neferhenut

I

II

III

IV

Princesses' catacombs

Causeway

Above: The plan of the complex of Senwosret III is heavily reminiscent of Third Dynasty practice, and represents a major shift from the practice of most of the previous millennium.

seems likely that they were actually removed from there. If so, they may have been installed as a concrete link with the earlier monument, which Senwosret III so clearly wished to recall in the design of his tomb. The Old Kingdom blocks used in Amenemhat I's pyramid may be analogues.

On the other hand, Djoser's pattern was not followed slavishly, there being no major temple on the north side of the pyramid, nor the '*Heb-sed*' complex seen there. Instead, in addition to the original eastern mortuary temple, there was a large temple in the (later) southern portion of the enclosure.

Senwosret III may also have revived the subsidiary pyramid. Pyramid 8 in the centre of the south face has just a single shaft with a small chamber that contains only an uninscribed canopic chest; clearly it was some kind of ritual structure.

The substructure of the pyramid was approached via a shaft

Left: The pyramid of Senwosret III; in the foreground is the corner of the outer enclosure wall.

on the west side. It is of a fairly simple form, similar to Fifth/Sixth Dynasty royal sepulchres. Interestingly, the granite walls of the burial chamber were whitewashed, contradicting the usual Egyptian practice of flaunting the use of hard stones.

It remains uncertain whether Senwosret III was ever buried in his pyramid: no traces of an interment were found, while the king, most unusually, had a second tomb at Abydos. This tomb at Abydos was of a highly unusual design, with no superstructure other than a temple, and is known to have been an important focus of the royal cult in later years.

Principal Explorations

The pyramid was examined by Perring in September/October 1839, and in the early 1880s Maspero made an unsuccessful attempt to enter it. Excavations were carried out by de Morgan in 1894, the pyramid being entered and important caches of jewellery found in the tombs of some of the king's daughters. Jéquier did some work on the causeway in 1924 before fresh excavations were begun by Arnold in 1990.

Arnold's work has greatly increased knowledge of the layout of the whole complex, and revealed another group of jewellery (see page 133).

Above: Senwosret III also had a funerary complex at Abydos, comprising a temple and town on the edge of cultivation, and then a complex under the edge of the cliffs. In the foreground can be seen the lines of walls that enclose an area dominated by a huge crater that marks the entrance to a rock-cut tomb. To the left, the two mounds are tombs S9 and S10 (see pages 103–4).

Right: Plan of the Abydos complex. Debate continues as to whether Senwosret III was buried there, rather than at Dahshur. The rock-cut tomb descends to a considerable depth, and has a number of features designed to deter thieves, including the concealment of the sarcophagus and canopic chest behind walling.

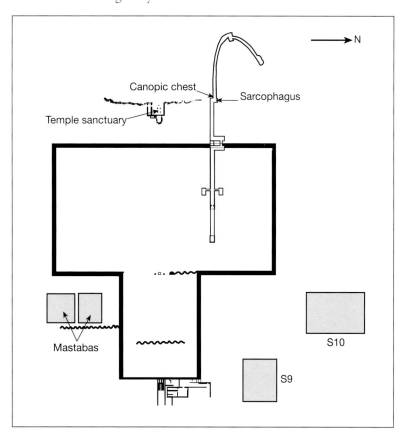

MODERN DESIGNATION:
L.LVIII; Black Pyramid
LOCATION: Dahshur
DATE: *c.* 1842–1794 BC
OWNER: Nimaatre
Amenemhat III
BASIS OF ATTRIBUTION:
Inscribed material from
complex
DIMENSIONS: Base 105
x 105 metres; recon-
structed height 75
metres

Right: Amenemhat III's Black Pyramid at Dahshur.

Below: Amenemhat III's pyramid plan shows a range of interesting features in the south-west quadrant.

AMENEMHAT III'S FIRST PYRAMID (BLACK PYRAMID)

A site due east of the Bent Pyramid was chosen for Amenemhat III's burial place. The brick pyramid itself, although badly ruined, remains a distinctive and impressive monument. The surviving part of the core is surrounded by heaps of pulverized, decomposed brickwork, some of it resulting from a major collapse during the 20th century. The elaborately decorated pyramidion survives in the Cairo Museum.

Here the pyramid complex reverts to a more standard form, although lacking any potential subsidiary pyramid. On the other hand, the substructure is more elaborate than before, with the tombs of two of the king's wives wholly within the pyramid's structure: Aat and an anonymous lady had chambers with their own entrances, but no separate superstructure. This complex was connected to the king's tomb chambers, with its own entrance on the opposite (west) side. For the first time pyramid entrance passages have stairs, greatly easing descent; in addition, the corridors have an average height of some 2 metres, contrasting with the low ceilings of Old Kingdom pyramids.

Plan labels:
N
Queens' burial chambers
South tomb
Tomb of Princess Nubhetepti-khered
Tomb of Hor
King's canopic room
King's burial chamber
Mortuary temple
Causeway

The king's main complex comprises a burial chamber near the centre of the pyramid, approached by a corridor flanked with store-rooms. Curiously, the canopic chest was intended to lie some 40 metres from the burial chamber. Apparently as a substitute for subsidiary pyramids for the king and his queens, a series of corridors were placed under the south face of the pyramid and equipped with chapels and three dummy canopic chests. These unique features were not revived in any pyramid.

The Black Pyramid's substructure displays numerous indications of structural failure, and the monument was not used for the king's burial, a new pyramid being built at Hawara (see below). However, the queens' interments do seem to have gone ahead, with further burial places improvised in the corridors and vestibules of the king's chambers. These improvised sepulchres may date to the Thirteenth Dynasty, when two shaft tombs on the north side were converted into royal tombs.

Principal Explorations

Examined by Perring in 1839, the complex was first excavated by de Morgan from December 1894 onwards; he first entered on 15 March 1895, having found the interior by means of tunnelling under the pyramid from the north. However, he neglected much of the enclosure, and the whole complex was re-excavated by Arnold from 1976 to 1983.

AMENEMHAT III'S SECOND PYRAMID

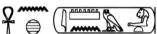 'Amenemhat Lives'

Having abandoned his original pyramid, Amenemhat III turned to the Fayoum for his new sepulchre. At Hawara, he erected a pyramid complex with several

Below: Amenemhat III's Second Pyramid at Hawara is also of radical design, incorporating a huge temple (the 'Labyrinth') on its south side. This partly restored plan is based on the extremely scanty traces that have survived into modern times.

MODERN DESIGNATION: L.LXVII
LOCATION: Hawara
DATE: c. 1842–1794 BC
OWNER: Nimaatre Amenemhat III
BASIS OF ATTRIBUTION: Inscribed material from complex
DIMENSIONS: Base 105 x 105 metres; reconstructed height 58 metres

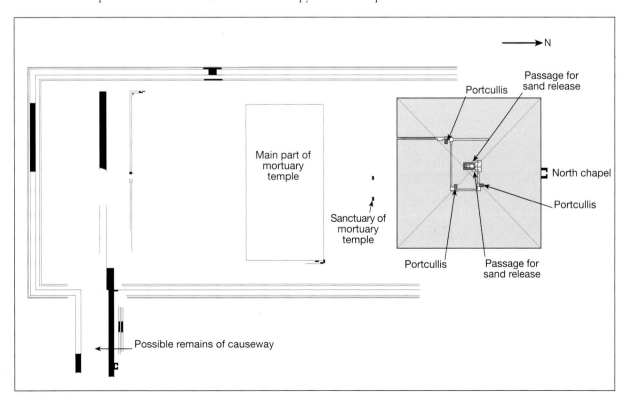

Above: The focus of the huge temple, the Labyrinth, of Amenemhat III's Second Pyramid at Hawara seems to have been a series of granite shrines near the south face of the pyramid; each shrine held two royal figures.

innovative features, and it is the best-preserved of the brick pyramids.

The temple complex lay predominantly on the south side of the pyramid itself, and covered an area of over 60,000 square metres. Subsequent destruction has made its plan difficult to work out, although its north part included a number of quartzite shrines, each with two royal figures inside. The entrance seems to have been in the south-east corner, and thus the whole structure may – like that of Senwosret III – be paying tribute to the pyramid complex of Djoser.

The entrance to the pyramid substructure is on the south side, and has even more elaborate protective devices than the Black Pyramid. Each change of direction is via a sliding quartzite portcullis slab in the ceiling, while the burial chamber is a single block of the same stone. Access was via a trench in the antechamber floor leading to a gap between the burial chamber's end wall and one of the roofing slabs, kept raised until the funeral. The slab was supported on props, bedded in a series of sand-filled 'chimneys'. The latter had plugs at the bottom: when these were removed, the sand would flow out, the props would sink down, and the slab would seal the chamber. Security was further enhanced by filling an apparently blind corridor near the pyramid entrance with stone blocks.

However, robbers mined the obstacles in the corridor and robbed the burial chamber; the king's body was burned. His granite sarcophagus, with the panelled lower part introduced in the previous reign, lay in the centre of the room, a canopic chest beyond its foot. An additional sarcophagus had been created by placing granite slabs between the east side of the king's sarcophagus and the wall, and adding a lid. An offering table in the room showed this extra sarcophagus to have been made for Princess Neferuptah. Her body was, however, removed prior to her father's death, and placed in a new pyramid, built two kilometres to the south (see page 134).

Principal Explorations

The mortuary temple was damaged early in the 19th century during the digging of the Wahbi Canal, which cut off a whole corner. It was examined by Perring on 1 November 1839 and first mapped by Lepsius in May–July 1843; it was excavated in 1888–9 and 1910 by Petrie, who is the only person to have entered the pyramid. Unable to find the entrance, he extended a robber's tunnel that ultimately led to the burial chamber; he then found the entrance by working his way outwards. Petrie was hindered by the rise of the water table since antiquity, which had filled many galleries with mud and water almost up to the ceiling. Subsequent increases in water levels meant that by the time the entrance was reopened by the Supreme Council for Antiquities in the 1990s, it was not possible to reach even the bottom of the entrance staircase.

The Thirteenth Dynasty

The tombs of the last two monarchs of the Twelfth Dynasty, Amenemhat IV and Queen Sobkneferu, are unknown. Our knowledge of the kings of the next dynasty is also very patchy and inconclusive. The Thirteenth Dynasty comprises a long series of monarchs who reigned for only short periods, and only a handful of them left known sepulchres. In addition, there are a number of pyramids of this date without identified owners. Accordingly, the ordering of these monuments is heavily reliant on the interpretation of the evolution of their architecture.

Two structures at Abydos may possibly be royal tombs of the Thirteenth Dynasty; they might reflect the shift in the dynasty's political mass southwards as Palestinian power built up in the delta. Ultimately, the Thirteenth Dynasty was to end with the takeover of northern Egypt by the 'Hyksos' Fifteenth Dynasty of Palestinian origin, an area ruled first by the Palestinian Fourteenth Dynasty. The Hyksos Fifteenth Dynasty seem to have violently displaced the earlier line *c.* 1650.

AMENEMHAT IV, V OR VI'S PYRAMID (?)

Near the ruined pyramid of Amenemhat II is an area of limestone rubble, some 40 metres square, with the line of a causeway leading from it. The rubble is probably the remains of a casing; together with the survival of the causeway, it suggests a considerable degree of completion at some stage.

Principal Explorations

No clearance has ever taken place, although the named fragment was recovered by Moussa in the 1970s; the site was damaged by pipe-laying in 1975.

MODERN DESIGNATION: L.LIV

LOCATION: Dahshur

DATE: *c.* 18th century BC

OWNER: Amenemhat IV, V or VI?

BASIS OF ATTRIBUTION: A fragment bearing the name Amenemhat was found in the area, although it might be a 'stray' piece from the nearby pyramid of Amenemhat II

DIMENSIONS: Base *c.* 40 metres square

Left: The wastes of South Dahshur were used as a royal necropolis, including the burial of Qemau, during the Thirteenth Dynasty. Qemau's Pyramid lay on a low hill at the right-hand end of this view. (see page 98).

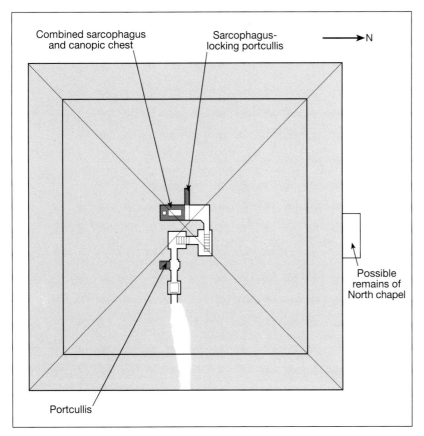

Combined sarcophagus and canopic chest

Sarcophagus-locking portcullis

→N

Possible remains of North chapel

Portcullis

QEMAU'S PYRAMID

Qemau's pyramid lies in an area previously used only for Old Kingdom private tombs. It was probably never finished; only some parts of the brickwork survive, and there are no certain remains of the complex apart from indications of a north chapel.

The inner part of the substructure, however, has survived, from the point where a large vertically sliding block prevented access through the ceiling of the vestibule at the bottom of the entrance passage into the rest of the tomb. From here a series of vestibules, closed off by a lateral portcullis, led to the burial chamber. The burial chamber embodied what is typologically the earliest of a new kind of combined sarcophagus/canopic chest, with cavities for both the body and its internal organs within the same block. This formed the floor of the room, and was sealed by a lid that was slid on top from the antechamber area directly north of the sarcophagus. The lid was locked into place by a sideways-sliding portcullis slab; as the lid was in contact with the chamber walls on three sides and the portcullis on the other, tomb-robbers had to resort to smashing the north end of the lid to gain access to the coffin, and then push the remains northwards to rifle the canopic cavity.

Principal Explorations

The site was cleared by Muses and Gabra in 1957, but the excavations were brought to a premature end that summer with Muses arrest for contravening antiquities law. Maragioglio and Rinaldi made an examination of the remains in the late 1960s.

TWO ANONYMOUS PYRAMIDS

Two possible ruined pyramids have been noted under the sand north-east and north-west of Qemau's monument. Nothing more is known.

Principal Explorations

First noticed by Arnold and Stadelmann in the mid-1970s.

MODERN DESIGNATION: Pyramid of Ameny-Qemau
LOCATION: Dahshur-South
DATE: 18th century BC
OWNER: (Ameny-) Qemau
BASIS OF ATTRIBUTION: The king's canopic jars found in the pyramid
DIMENSIONS: Base 53 x 53 metres

Above: The substructure of Qemau's pyramid had a number of security features, including a combined sarcophagus and canopic chest whose lid was locked in place by a lateral portcullis.

MODERN DESIGNATION: A & B
LOCATION: Dahshur-South
DATE: 18th century BC
OWNER: Not known
BASIS OF ATTRIBUTION: Location in an area otherwise known to have been used during the Thirteenth Dynasty
DIMENSIONS: Not known

THE NORTH PYRAMID OF MAZGHUNA

The early Thirteenth Dynasty royal necropolis spread further southward from Dahshur to Mazghuna, where two pyramids have been found. Although a very thick layer of limestone chips covered its site, the northern pyramid was entirely destroyed before 1910. Nothing of the core was then traceable, although Lepsius included it on his map. In view of the lack of any brick debris, it is possible that the structure may have been of stone, unlike preceding pyramids. The only part of the complex that has been traced in detail is a 116-metre section of the foundations of the exceptionally wide causeway.

The actual entrance to the pyramid has been destroyed, the first preserved part being steps descending from the north. However, since the size of the pyramid is very uncertain, it is not clear where the actual entrance was. In contrast to the state of the superstructure, the roofing of the rest of the substructure is intact, the plan being reminiscent of that of Qemau, albeit with additions; the arrangement of the combined sarcophagus/canopic chest, portcullis and antechamber is exactly the same. It seems likely that the pyramid had never been used for a burial, as the sarcophagus lid was found still stored in the antechamber.

Principal Explorations

Examined by Lepsius in spring 1843 and entered by de Morgan in the 1890s, the pyramid was cleared by Mackay in 1910–11.

THE TOMB OF HOR

The Tomb of Hor has been dated to the middle of the Thirteenth Dynasty. It is an enlarged version of a simple shaft tomb on the north side of Amenemhat III's Black Pyramid, with the addition of a new stone burial chamber. Except for the omission of a portcullis and the use of a

Right: Plan of the North Pyramid of Mazghuna. This pyramid has the widest known causeway, but a totally destroyed superstructure. Its dimensions could vary anywhere between the two potential baselines shown. A mound just north of the causeway may represent a queen's pyramid.

MODERN DESIGNATION: L.LIX; North Pyramid
LOCATION: Mazghuna
DATE: 18th century BC
OWNER: A later king than Qemau
BASIS OF ATTRIBUTION: Slightly more developed than Qemau's pyramid
DIMENSIONS: Base *c.* 58 metres square?

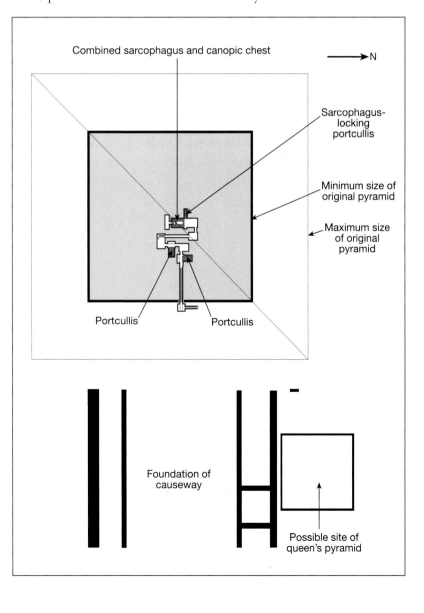

Combined sarcophagus and canopic chest

N

Sarcophagus-locking portcullis

Minimum size of original pyramid

Maximum size of original pyramid

Portcullis

Portcullis

Foundation of causeway

Possible site of queen's pyramid

separate sarcophagus and canopic chest, the arrangement mirrors that found in contemporary pyramids (e.g. Qemau's). The existence of this tomb suggests that other kings of the period may have had similar sepulchres, explaining why there are so few known pyramids in relation to the number of kings.

The great interest of this tomb derives from the fact that it suffered relatively lightly at the hands of the tomb-robbers, thus providing us with our only sizeable body of information on what accompanied a Middle Kingdom monarch to the grave. The antechamber contained principally a celebrated ka-statue in its shrine, two alabaster stelae, one with an offering formula, a case for staves, and a number of pottery and (dummy) wooden vessels. Inside his sarcophagus, the king's rifled body lay within a badly decayed rectangular coffin, decorated with an eye-panel and inscribed gold strips.

Although stripped of much of his finery, Hor retained some of his equipment: his once-gilded mask, and the remains of two falcon collars and a dagger. The mummy itself had been reduced to a damaged skeleton. Alongside him lay a stave, two long sceptres, an inlaid flail, two small alabaster vases and a wooden mallet. The wooden inner canopic chest, which closely matched the coffin and still contained four human-headed canopic jars, was found still sealed.

Principal Explorations
The tomb was discovered by de Morgan on 16 April 1894.

THE SOUTH PYRAMID OF MAZGHUNA
This brick monument lies some 400 metres from the North Pyramid. The pyramid itself has been entirely destroyed, along with much of the roofing of the substructure; only a thin coating of limestone chips marked the site. The brick enclosure wall was of a wavy form, with a simple mortuary temple of the same material on the east side; another structure in the south-east corner of the enclosure seems to have been some form of gatehouse, through which the pyramid itself could be approached. Quarry marks indicate that work was being carried on in the third year of an unnamed king.

The outer part of the descending corridor is lost, but the corridor gives access to the interior via two granite portcullises of a design and workmanship identical with that seen in the North Pyramid. The arrangement of the innermost part is reminiscent of that found in Amenemhat III's Second Pyramid at Hawara, but with the difference that the chamber, sarcophagus and

Below: Plan of the South Pyramid of Mazghuna, showing the 'wavy' enclosure wall and small brick chapel.

MODERN DESIGNATION: South Pyramid
LOCATION: Mazghuna
DATE: 18th century BC
OWNER: Not known
BASIS OF ATTRIBUTION: No inscribed material found; on the basis of design, the pyramid is later than the North Pyramid, but earlier than that of Khendjer
DIMENSIONS: Base 52 x 52 metres

Portcullises

Burial chamber with integral sarcophagus and canopic chest

N →

Mortuary temple

canopic chest are now made from a single block. Compared with earlier sarcophagus/canopic chests, the block was considerably deeper, leaving a considerable void above the cavities for the coffin and canopic vessels, while a straightforward lid was abandoned in favour of two more massive blocks. One block was intended as a fixture, cut away below to give additional head-room for the burial party, but the other was supported by a pair of quartzite props, equipped with 'sandraulics' like the Hawara pyramid. The whole arrangement is thus a cross between that found in the North Pyramid and Qemau's Pyramid on one hand, and that of the Hawara pyramid on the other. The burial chamber had been broken open by pushing the entrance block northwards, having demolished the southern wall of the antechamber: only a fragment of a make-up pot and an inlay survived when the pyramid was excavated.

Principal Explorations
Identified and cleared by Mackay in 1910–11.

KHENDJER'S PYRAMID
The enclosure seems originally to have had the same 'wavy' wall as the South Pyramid at Mazghuna, but this was then replaced with a niched one of stone. Remains of an eastern mortuary temple and a north chapel have both been located. It is known that the pyramid was completed, as fragments of the pyramidion were found nearby.

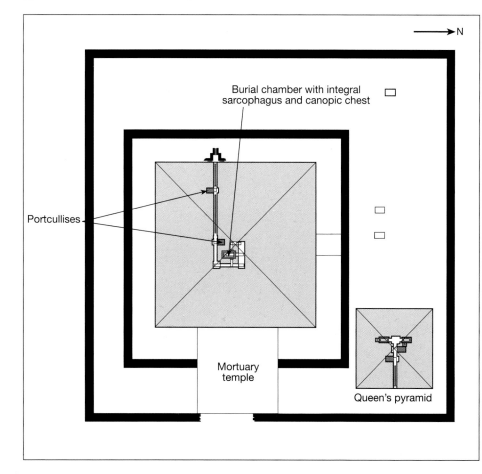

Burial chamber with integral sarcophagus and canopic chest

N

Portcullises

Mortuary temple

Queen's pyramid

Left: The pyramid complex of Khendjer in southern Saqqara-South, with its Queen's pyramid in the north-east corner.

MODERN DESIGNATION: L.XLIV

LOCATION: Southern Saqqara-South

DATE: 18th century BC

OWNER: Userkare Khendjer

BASIS OF ATTRIBUTION: Inscribed pyramidion

DIMENSIONS: Base 53 x 53 metres; height 37 metres

Right: The cap-stone of Khendjer's Pyramid is now on display in the Cairo Museum.

Internally, the structure represents a further development of the arrangements found in the South Pyramid of Mazghuna.

Principal Explorations

The site was visited by Lepsius in 1843. The pyramid was entered by de Morgan during the 1890s and excavated by Jéquier in 1929–31.

PYRAMID OF AN UNKNOWN KING

MODERN DESIGNATION: L.XLVI; Unfinished Pyramid
LOCATION: Southern Saqqara-South
DATE: 18th century BC
OWNER: Unknown king
BASIS OF ATTRIBUTION: The elaboration and scale of the monument would suggest that it is the latest of the known Middle Kingdom pyramids
DIMENSIONS: Base 91 x 91 metres

The fifth excavated pyramid of the Thirteenth Dynasty lies just south of Khendjer's Pyramid, and was apparently never finished. As well as being by far the largest pyramid of the dynasty, its substructure is one of the most elaborate of any Egyptian sepulchral monument, with a series of vestibules, changes of level and portcullises. One of its most remarkable features is its two burial chambers. The principal one was carved out of a block of quartzite, with a conventional-looking sarcophagus and canopic chest within, but carved as one with the chamber. Closure of the chamber was to be by the now customary 'sandraulic' means, but the tomb was never used.

The other burial chamber lay to the west and had an arrangement of sarcophagus/lid/portcullis similar to Qemau's, but reversed, with a separate canopic chest. The chamber has been described as a queen's, but no equivalent installation is known elsewhere. Given the elaboration of the substructure, which was clearly inspired by the desire for security, the most attractive solution is that it was actually a decoy, intended to draw plunderers away from the real burial.

Right: The antechamber of the Unfinished Pyramid: the upper doorway leads to the dummy burial chamber, while the opening contains a shaft used by those triggering the 'sandraulic' sealing system for the burial chamber. The burial chamber is beyond the left-hand wall.

Principal Explorations

The site was visited by Lepsius in 1843. The pyramid was entered by de Morgan during the 1890s and excavated by Jéquier in 1929–31.

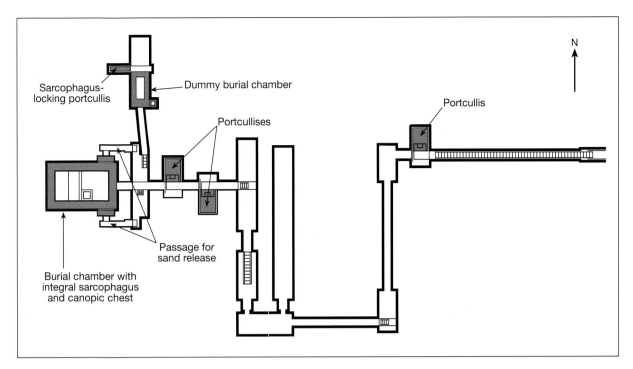

ABYDOS TOMB S9

Back in the Twelfth Dynasty, a large temple-tomb complex had been built in the southern part of the Abydos cemetery for Senwosret III (see page 91). Two tombs, with their superstructures largely destroyed, lie just north-east of this structure, and it has been suggested that the forms of their substructures may mark them out as royal tombs of the Thirteenth Dynasty – whether or not their superstructures were mastabas or pyramids.

This sepulchre employs the twisting, quartzite portcullis-blocked plan seen in all the pyramids of the dynasty, together with the combined burial chamber/sarcophagus/canopic chest typified by the pyramid of Khendjer. However, in the case of S9 no 'sandraulics' were employed: lowering of portcullises and the access block

Above: Plan of the substructure of the Unfinished Pyramid at Saqqara-South, the most elaborate example to be found in any pyramid.

MODERN DESIGNATION: S9

LOCATION: Abydos

DATE: 18th century BC

OWNER: King of the later Thirteenth Dynasty (?)

BASIS OF ATTRIBUTION: Similarity in design of substructure to other royal tombs of the dynasty

DIMENSIONS: Not known

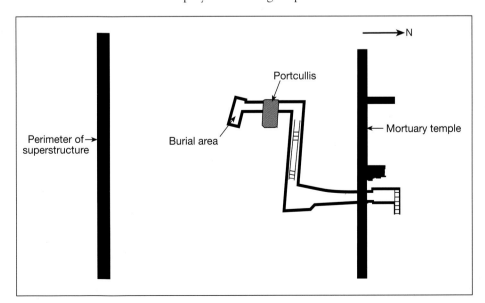

Left: Tomb S9 at Abydos; its location is shown on page 93. Its substructure design is similar to those of the Thirteenth Dynasty.

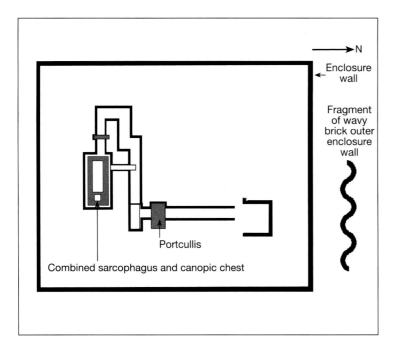

N

Enclosure wall

Fragment of wavy brick outer enclosure wall

Portcullis

Combined sarcophagus and canopic chest

Above: Tomb S10 at Abydos. As with Tomb S9 on page 103, this could be a royal tomb from the Thirteenth Dynasty.

Below: The pyramidion of the lost pyramid of Iy was found in the Nile delta, but is now in the Cairo Museum.

of the burial chamber was apparently done by the manual removal of the supports. In the case of the burial chamber block, this was done by means of a narrow service passage (only 50 centimetres wide by 55 centimetres high) from the approach corridor; perhaps owing to the constriction, the job was botched, leaving the burial chamber partly open.

Only some elements of the mudbrick complex survive, including what may be sections of the chapel and inner enclosure. Part of a 'wavy' outer enclosure wall has also been traced.

Principal Explorations

The tomb was partly cleared by Amélineau in 1896, and then excavated by Weigall in 1901–1902. Further work is planned.

ABYDOS TOMB S10

This tomb is less regular than S9, more badly damaged, and seems to have lacked an integrated burial chamber. Indeed, although a huge quartzite sarcophagus lid remains, no coffer survives; the coffer may have been of limestone. On the other hand, a typical late Middle Kingdom stairway flanked with benches is to be found in the main corridor of the tomb. A fragment of canopic jar was found.

MODERN DESIGNATION: S10
LOCATION: Abydos
DATE: 18th century BC
OWNER: King of the later Thirteenth Dynasty?
BASIS OF ATTRIBUTION: Similarity in design of substructure to other royal tombs of the dynasty
DIMENSIONS: Not known

Principal Explorations

The tomb was excavated by Weigall in 1901–1902. Further work is planned.

IY'S PYRAMID

Only the pyramidion of this tomb has been found (Cairo Museum TR 5/1/15/12). It came from Kataana in the delta, but it is likely that it was taken there as booty by the Hyksos kings. In contrast to the elaborate pyramidia of Amenemhat III and Khendjer, it merely bears an image of the king offering to Ptah.

MODERN DESIGNATION: None
LOCATION: Uncertain
DATE: c. 1700 BC
OWNER: Merneferre Iy
BASIS OF ATTRIBUTION: Pyramidion bears king's name
DIMENSIONS: Not known

THE SECOND INTERMEDIATE PERIOD

The Thirteenth Dynasty's grasp on power seems gradually to have slipped until, around 1650 BC, the whole of Lower (northern) Egypt came under the rule of the Palestinian Hyksos Fifteenth Dynasty. The full extent of their power is still the subject of debate, but there is evidence that their nominal power stretched a long way into the south, possibly embracing even Thebes for a relatively short period.

Below: Western Thebes, with Deir el-Bahari on the left and the southern end of Dira Abu'l-Naga on the right.

While the Palestinians ruled in the north, the rump of the old royal line moved south to Thebes, where it is now referred to as the Sixteenth/Seventeenth Dynasty. At Thebes the native Egyptian line initiated the royal cemetery at Dira Abu'l-Naga. There, they erected what – with one exception – were to be the last kings' pyramids to be built in Egypt.

Below: Dira Abu'l-Naga, the royal necropolis of the Seventeenth Dynasty. After the abandonment of pyramids by royalty, some private individuals began to place pyramids above their rock-cut chapels. The remains of some of these lie high up the slope to the right. In the distance is El-Qurn, the natural pyramid that towers above the New Kingdom Valley of the Kings (see pages 112–13).

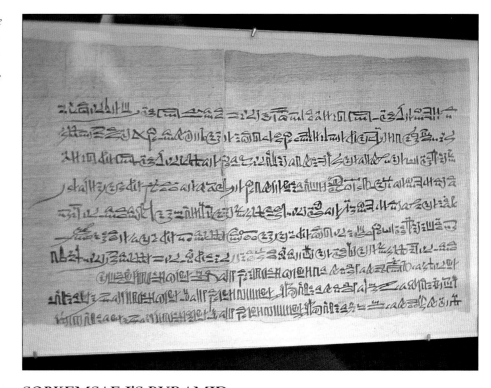

SOBKEMSAF I'S PYRAMID

MODERN DESIGNATION:
None
LOCATION: Dira Abu'l-Naga
DATE: Early 16th century BC
OWNER: Sekhemre-shedtawi Sobkemsaf I
BASIS OF ATTRIBUTION: Known only from Abbott Papyrus
DIMENSIONS: Not known

In Year 16 of the Twentieth Dynasty, Pharaoh Rameses IX (*c.* 1100 BC) appointed a commission to investigate claims that a number of royal tombs had been robbed. Ten royal sepulchres were accordingly examined, six of them being Seventeenth Dynasty kings' pyramids at Dira Abu'l-Naga.

The report of the commission, the Abbott Papyrus, now in the British Museum, is our sole source of information on three of the pyramids, including the pyramid of Sobkemsaf I. Sobkemsaf I's burial chamber was stated to have been found 'without its lord' and his queen, 'thieves having laid hands on them'. The robbers were later apprehended. The transcript of the trial of the robbers, including their confession, is in the Leopold II-Amherst Papyrus, which is now split between Brussels and New York:

> *We found the pyramid of King Sobkemsaf I, this being unlike the pyramids and tombs of the nobles that we were used to rob. We took our copper tools and forced a way into the pyramid of this king through its innermost part. We found the substructure, and we took our lighted candles in our hands and went down. Then we broke through the blocking that we found at the entrance to his crypt, and found this god lying at the back of his burial place. And we found the burial-place of Queen Nubkhaes, his wife, situated beside him, it being protected and guarded by plaster and enclosed by a stone blocking. This we also broke through, and found her resting there in the same way.*
>
> *We opened their sarcophagi and their coffins in which they were, and found the noble mummy of this king equipped with a khepesh-sword; many amulets and jewels were upon his neck, and his headpiece of gold was upon him. The noble mummy of the king was completely bedecked with gold, and his coffins were adorned with gold and silver inside and out and inlaid with all kinds of precious stones ...*

INYOTEF V'S PYRAMID

The ancient commission found an incomplete tunnel being made into Inyotef V's pyramid. The pyramid's steep angle of elevation is shown by the surviving cap-stone, now in the British Museum. This cap-stone bore the king's names, and also those of his parents. Unfortunately, the parents' names were largely destroyed when the upper and lower parts of the cap-stone were broken away.

Nothing else is known of the pyramid's superstructure, but the entrance to the substructure seems to have been a brick-lined pit, about 20 feet deep, halfway up the Dira Abu'l-Naga hill. From the entrance pit a corridor led to a chamber in which two coffins lay, 'covered with cloth and dirt thrown over them', according to the local plunderers who found them in modern times. Both coffins are now in the Louvre Museum: one was that of Inyotef V himself, the other a private coffin, hurriedly adapted to hold the body of King Sekhemreheruhirmaet Inyotef (VII). The latter seems to have been the next-but-one king, buried in a recent predecessor's tomb after the briefest of reigns. Inyotef V's canopic chest, presumably found with the coffin, is also in the Louvre, Paris.

Principal Explorations

The tomb has never been scientifically located and investigated, but local plunderers penetrated the substructure in the late 1840s. Their testimony was recorded by Wilkinson between 1849 and 1855.

MODERN DESIGNATION: None
LOCATION: Dira Abu'l-Naga
DATE: Early 16th century BC
OWNER: Sekhemre-wep-maat Inyotef V
BASIS OF ATTRIBUTION: Abbott Papyrus; items of funerary equipment
DIMENSIONS: Not known

Above: The pyramidion from the tomb of Inyotef V in Dira Abu'l-Naga can now be found in the British Museum.

Left: The coffins of Inyotef VII (left) and Inyotef V, from the latter's burial chamber, are on display in the Louvre, Paris.

INYOTEF VI'S PYRAMID

MODERN DESIGNATION:
None

LOCATION: Dira Abu'l-
Naga

DATE: Early 16th centu-
ry BC

OWNER: Nubkheperre
Inyotef VI

BASIS OF ATTRIBUTION:
Abbott Papyrus;
inscribed material

DIMENSIONS: Base 11 x
11 metres; restored
height 13 metres

*Below: The site of the
pyramid of Inyotef VI lies
on the slope directly behind
the modern shelter; this
shelter protects the entrance
to the tomb-chapel of
Shuroy (TT13).*

Inyotef VI's pyramid is the only one of these Second Intermediate Period pyramids to have been properly investigated in modern times. The white-plastered brick pyramid was built on the slope of the hill, its sides rising at an angle of between 65 and 68 degrees; a pair of obelisks bearing the king's name stood outside the chapel. The burial chamber was reached by a shaft cut in the bedrock in front of the south-east corner of the pyramid. The room, with a high ceiling, had a cutting in the floor to contain the coffin. The coffin is now in the British Museum.

Principal Explorations

Although an attempt had been made under Rameses IX to tunnel into the tomb from the tomb-chapel of Shuroy (see picture below), the burial chamber seems to have remained intact until 1827. It was then entered by local plunderers, who removed the coffin and mummy, apparently destroying the latter through carelessness. The coffin was then sold to the British Consul, Henry Salt, and later purchased as part of Salt's collection by the British Museum.

Mariette rediscovered the pyramid in 1860, but failed to publish any details. The obelisks were removed by Maspero in 1881; sadly, both pieces were lost in the Nile en route to Cairo.

The site was then lost until 1919–20 when Winlock identified the tomb, which the Abbott Papyrus indicates as being the start of a robber's tunnel heading for the pyramid. Finally, in 2001, Polz used the same data to locate the pyramid directly next to the tomb of Shuroy (TT13).

TAA I'S PYRAMID

The king's tomb was found untouched by Rameses IX's commissioners; their report suggests that his tomb was near the southern end of Dira Abu'l-Naga. Taa I's mummy and coffin have never come to light.

MODERN DESIGNATION: None
LOCATION: Dira Abu'l-Naga
DATE: Mid-16th century BC
OWNER: Senakhtenre Taa I
BASIS OF ATTRIBUTION: Known only from Abbott Papyrus
DIMENSIONS: Not known

TAA II'S PYRAMID

Although found untouched by Rameses IX's commissioners, the king's mummy and coffin were later removed for reburial. The king's mummy showed severe head wounds, suggesting death in battle. The mummy and coffin were ultimately placed in the tomb of the High Priest Pinudjem II near Deir el-Bahari (TT320), some time after Year 11 of Shoshenq I (*c.* 932 BC); found there in 1881, they are now in the Cairo Museum.

MODERN DESIGNATION: None
LOCATION: Dira Abu'l-Naga
DATE: *c.* 1558–1553 BC
OWNER: Seqenenre Taa II
BASIS OF ATTRIBUTION: Known only from Abbott Papyrus
DIMENSIONS: Not known

Above: The horrific head wounds that caused the death of Taa II, and which were probably inflicted during a battle against the Hyksos, are still visible on Taa II's mummified head, now in the Cairo Museum.

KAMOSE'S PYRAMID

Similarly found untouched by Rameses IX's commissioners, the king's mummy and coffin were also later removed and found buried in debris near the mouth of the Valley of the Kings. Discovered in 1857, the coffin is now in the Cairo Museum, although the mummy crumbled to dust. The Abbott Papyrus implies that Kamose's pyramid was the southernmost in the cemetery, and, near the likely spot, Winlock discovered a small pyramid that he believed could be that of the king. The identification is not, however, in any way certain.

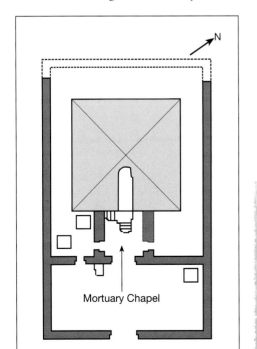

Mortuary Chapel

MODERN DESIGNATION: None
LOCATION: Dira Abu'l-Naga
DATE: *c.* 1553–1549 BC
OWNER: Wadjkheperre Kamose
BASIS OF ATTRIBUTION: Known from Abbott Papyrus, which implies its location at the southern end of Dira Abu'l-Naga
DIMENSIONS: Not known

Left: Plan of a small pyramid at the southern end of Dira Abu'l-Naga which has occasionally been attributed to Kamose.

THE EVOLUTION OF THE PYRAMID: THE NEW KINGDOM ONWARDS

Below: The tombs were generally elaborately decorated, with the 'Books of the Underworld' and depictions of the king before the gods. This is the tomb of Horemheb (KV57).

The reunification of Egypt around 1550 BC marked a major change in royal funerary practices, which would soon end 1,000 years of pyramid-building for the tombs of the Egyptian kings, although there would be a short-lived revival some eight centuries later.

THE NEW KINGDOM

One final pyramid was erected, however, by the first king of the Eighteenth Dynasty, Ahmose I. Ahmose had been responsible for the final expulsion of the Palestinian Hyksos Fifteenth Dynasty and the re-establishment of royal power. The succeeding kings established Egyptian hegemony over much of Syria–Palestine, with the height of Egyptian power coming under Amenhotep III. A gradual decline followed Amenhotep III's reign, exacerbated by conflicts within the royal family during the late Nineteenth Dynasty and economic difficulties in the Twentieth Dynasty.

AHMOSE I'S PYRAMID

Ahmose I built a funerary monument a few hundred metres south of Senwosret III's Abydene complex; as with that monument, it is uncertain whether Ahmose I's was actually used for a burial or – more likely – was a cenotaph. Ahmose I's complex comprises a number of elements. First, a rubble-cored, but limestone-sheathed, pyramid stands near the boundary between desert and cultivated land; its angle one can assume to have been 63 degrees. A temple adjoining its east side was once decorated with extensive, but now fragmentary, battle scenes, perhaps recording the king's defeat of the Hyksos; a smaller chapel lies just to the north. At the opposite end of the complex's 1.4-kilometre axis, further into the desert, was another temple, rising in terraces against the cliff face. In the expanse of desert between the pyramid and the temple, Ahmose constructed two monuments. The first was a brick chapel dedicated to the king's grandmother, Tetisherit, containing a fine stela, now in the Cairo Museum. The second was a subterranean tomb of unusual form. It is cut for the most part only a few metres below the surface; a pit entrance gives access to a twisting passageway that eventually opens into a great hall, its roof formerly supported by 18 columns. Below the hall, a further passage, probably unfinished, leads deeper into the matrix.

MODERN DESIGNATION: Kom el-Sheikh Mohammed
LOCATION: Abydos
DATE: c. 1549–1524 BC
OWNER: Nebpehtyre Ahmose I
BASIS OF ATTRIBUTION: Inscribed material from the complex
DIMENSIONS: Base 80 x 80 metres

Left: The pyramid of Ahmose I at Abydos is the last such monument built by a native king of Egypt. No passages are known within the pyramid, and the substructure lies far out in the desert beyond the monument.

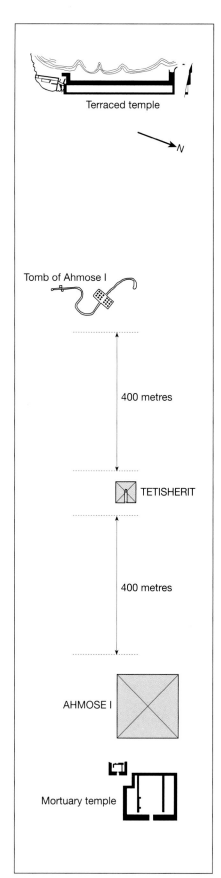

Terraced temple

N

Tomb of Ahmose I

400 metres

TETISHERIT

400 metres

AHMOSE I

Mortuary temple

Little was found by the excavators: only a few bricks, stamped with Ahmose's praenomen, and a number of fragments of gold leaf came to light in the debris of the pillared hall. An interesting point is that the pyramid's core contained rubble from the construction of the tomb.

Principal Explorations

Although Amélineau seems to have examined the area in 1896, the pyramid was first excavated by Mace in 1899–1900, and the rest of the complex by Currelly in 1902, the substructure being discovered through the clue supplied by the hollow in the ground created by the pillared hall's collapse. New investigations were begun by Harvey in 1993.

The Eclipse of the Pyramid

Ahmose I's pyramid was the last pyramid to be built by a native Egyptian king – the last of a line stretching back over 1,000 years to Djoser and Imhotep. His successors, beginning with Thutmose I, revived the Archaic Period practice of separating the burial chamber from the offering place. The latter was set near the desert edge at Thebes, in the form of a large mortuary – or rather 'memorial' –

Left: Plan of the Ahmose I complex at Abydos, with his mortuary temple, his pyramid, the pyramidal chapel of the royal grandmother, Tetisherit, the subterranean tomb and the terraced temple against the cliffs.

Below: Once kings had ceased to use pyramids, they began to be adopted by rapidly descending echelons of the social ladder. This example, at Deir el-Medina, belonged to one of the workmen employed on building the royal tombs in the Valley of the Kings during the Nineteenth Dynasty.

Left: The Valley of the Kings, burial place of the kings of the New Kingdom. This site has been a tourist attraction since Roman times, visitors being attracted to the beautifully carved and painted galleries as well as to the frisson of mystery that surrounds royal sepulchres. The tomb in the centre is that of Rameses VI. During the Twentieth Dynasty, efforts to hide the royal tombs were abandoned in favour of impressive gateways.

temple, while the substructure lay over a kilometre away behind a curtain of cliffs in what has come to be known as the Valley of the Kings. There, galleries penetrated deep into the bedrock, resurrecting ancient practice by bearing the decoration that is the ultimate descendant of the Pyramid Texts. But there was no pyramid erected over the offering place or burial place. Indeed, the pyramid now became the marker for the tombs of private individuals: small brick structures built above the rock-chapels along the front of the Theban necropolis. Yet, in one sense, kings continued to rest under a pyramid: for over the Valley of the Kings rears El-Qurn, the sacred mountain home of the goddess Mertseger, 'the Lover of Silence', and the most magnificent of all natural pyramids.

THE THIRD INTERMEDIATE AND LATE PERIODS

The Valley of the Kings accommodated royal tombs until the end of the Twentieth Dynasty. After this, around 1070 BC, with the foundation of the Twenty-first Dynasty, the capital of Egypt moved north to Tanis (San el-Hagar) in the delta. Tanis lies many miles from any place suitable for rock-cut monuments, and accordingly the new royal cemetery comprised stone-built structures sunk just below the ground surface, and probably topped by chapels. These tombs are of modest dimensions, containing at most a handful of chambers and generally decorated with books of the underworld.

Below: With the Third Intermediate Period, the royal cemeteries moved to the north, where they comprised stone chambers sunk in the soil of temple courtyards. Here, at Tanis, we have the tombs of Pasebkhanu I and Osorkon II (NRT-III and I).

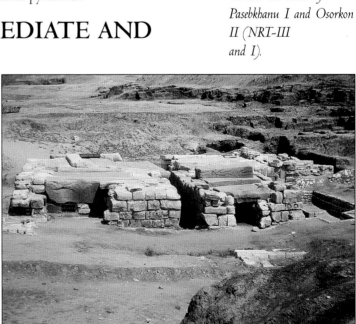

The Tanite tombs lay in the forecourt of the city's principal temple, and after Thebes effectively became an independent polity in the middle of the Twenty-second Dynasty, at least one king had a tomb within the temple complex of Medinet Habu there. Similar tomb locations were used for nearly all later known royal cemeteries, although the physical remains of only one such sepulchre, of Nefarud I at Mendes (Twenty-ninth Dynasty), has been examined.

Resurrection in Sudan: the Twenty-fifth Dynasty

The exception to the rule of temple burial comes from the Twenty-fifth Dynasty. The latter part of the Third Intermediate Period saw increasing fragmentation of Egypt, reversed only with the annexation of the country by the Egyptianized rulers of Sudan (Kush). Although buried in their home country, these kings resumed the use of pyramids, albeit of the steeply angled type used by the Seventeenth Dynasty kings, and later nobles, at Thebes.

PI(ANKH)YE'S PYRAMID

The pyramid of Piye is wholly vanished, together with the chapel. However, the substructure still survives, consisting of a corbel-roofed room approached by a stairway. Although sets of canopic jars and *shabtis* (see glossary, page 139) were provided, instead of a sarcophagus a rock-cut bench lay in the middle of the burial chamber with a cut-out in each corner to receive the legs of a bed. Interment on a bier has been characterized as a typical feature of Nubian burials since Kerman (Second Intermediate Period) times.

Principal Explorations
Excavated by Reisner in 1918–19.

MODERN DESIGNATION: Ku17

LOCATION: El-Kurru

DATE: *c.* 752–717 BC

OWNER: Seneferre Pi(ankh)ye

BASIS OF ATTRIBUTION: Funerary figure with name of king

DIMENSIONS: Base 8 x 8 metres

Right: *The remains of the corbelled roof of the burial chamber of Pi(ankh)ye at El-Kurru (Ku17).*

SHABAKA'S PYRAMID

Also entirely destroyed above ground, Shabaka's tomb displays rather better workmanship than Piye's, both in its architecture — which is fully rock-cut — and its funerary equipment, which includes a fine set of canopic jars. The burial chamber also preserves traces of paintings.

Principal Explorations
Excavated by Reisner in 1918–19.

SHABATAKA'S PYRAMID

The sepulchre of Shabataka marks something of a regression. The workmanship of his canopics is poor, while the burial chamber reverts to corbelled roofing; the tomb also has an unusual right-angled turn in its descending stairway. The tomb lies apart from the other Twenty-fifth Dynasty sepulchres, and is among the burial places of the ancestors of the royal line which date perhaps as far back as the early Third Intermediate Period.

Principal Explorations
Excavated by Reisner in 1918–19.

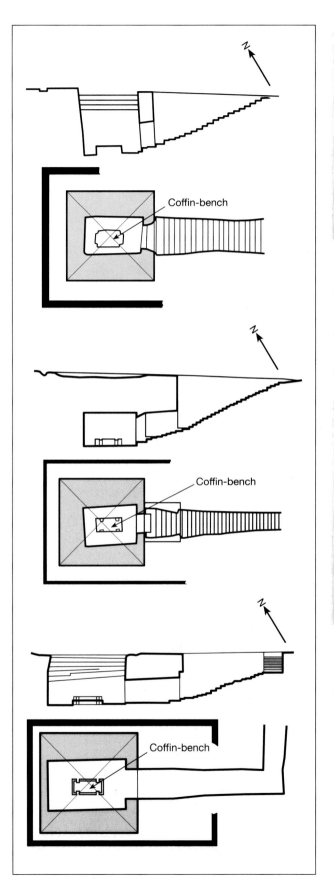

Left: Sections and plans of the pyramids of P(iankh)ye, Shabaka and Shabataka; they were far smaller than any king's pyramid of earlier periods.

MODERN DESIGNATION: Ku15
LOCATION: El-Kurru
DATE: *c.* 717–703 BC
OWNER: Neferkare Shabaka
BASIS OF ATTRIBUTION: Various inscribed items
DIMENSIONS: Base 11 x 11 metres

MODERN DESIGNATION: Ku18
LOCATION: El-Kurru
DATE: *c.* 703–690 BC
OWNER: Djedkare Shabataka
BASIS OF ATTRIBUTION: Funerary figure with name of king
DIMENSIONS: Base 11 x 11 metres

Coffin-bench

Coffin-bench

Coffin-bench

MODERN DESIGNATION:
Nu1
LOCATION: Nuri
DATE: *c.* 690–664 BC
OWNER: Khunefertumre
Taharqa
BASIS OF ATTRIBUTION
Substructure contained
large amounts of funer-
ary equipment bearing
his name.
DIMENSIONS: Base 52 x
52 metres

Right: Although now badly
ruined, Taharqa's pyramid
at Nuri is the largest of all
the Sudanese monuments.

Below: Plans of the
pyramids of Taharqa
and Tanutamun.

TAHARQA'S PYRAMID

Rather than make use of the now somewhat crowded family cemetery of
El-Kurru, Taharqa made a fresh start at Nuri, a little way downstream. His
pyramid was built in two phases, the first having a 29.5-metre base, with which the
substructure was aligned; the final version had a different axis. Apart from its size,
with a base nearly seven times that of the monument of Piye, Taharqa's pyramid
has the most elaborate substructure of
any Kushite royal tomb. A conventional
stairway, over which a mortuary chapel
may have been built, led into a small
antechamber, which in turn gave access
to a six-pillared burial chamber with
vaulted aisles. A curious corridor
completely surrounded the subterranean rooms at a slightly higher level,
accessible via a flight of steps at the far
end of the sepulchral chamber, or a pair
of stairways just outside the doorway of
the antechamber. The usual bench lay in
the centre of the burial chamber; the
nest of coffins that had lain on this had
been largely destroyed, but quantities of
their gold foil and stone inlay remained,
plus a fragment of skull.

The canopic jars are of a very fine
quality, and introduce new textual
formulations, which became standard
in subsequent Egyptian burials. A vast

Coffin-bench

number of *shabtis* were recovered in a variety of hard and soft stones, and many in remarkably large sizes – up to 60 centimetres in height.

Principal Explorations
Excavated by Reisner in 1918–19.

TANUTAMUN'S PYRAMID
The last Kushite to rule Egypt was Tanutamun. For his pyramid site he moved back to El-Kurru, adopting a much simpler substructure, curiously without the previously obligatory coffin-bench. Like Shabaka's tomb, Tanutamun's had a burial chamber adorned with paintings, in his case sufficiently well preserved to identify the topics covered. The vignettes and texts essentially follow the age-old association of royal burials with solar matters, the entrance doorway being surmounted by painted apes adoring the sun-god in his bark; a similar motif appears on the rear wall.

Principal Explorations
Excavated by Reisner in 1918–19.

Later Kushite Pyramids
Tanutamun's rule in Egypt ended with an Assyrian invasion in 656 BC. However, his successors continued to rule in what is modern Sudan for centuries more. Pyramids also continued to be built, although their contents and ornamentation show a steady shift towards a distinctly Kushite interpretation of the ancient motifs. Canopic jars initially remained in use, supplemented for a short period by (for the first time in Kush) stone sarcophagi, but both types of container had disappeared soon after the reign of Melanaqeñ, sixth successor of Tanutamun. At first the royal tombs were primarily built at Nuri, but they later shifted further south to Gebel Barkal and Meroë. It was at Meroë that the last Nilotic pyramid was built, around AD 350, 3,000 years and 1,600 kilometres from the first such monument at Saqqara.

MODERN DESIGNATION: Ku16
LOCATION: El-Kurru
DATE: 664–*c.* 656 BC
OWNER: Bakare Tanutamun
BASIS OF ATTRIBUTION: Decoration of burial chamber and inscribed material
DIMENSIONS: Base 8.25 x 8.25 metres

Below: *Sudanese pyramids, including these examples at Nuri, have a particularly high angle of elevation, apparently copied from the royal and private pyramids at Thebes.*

THE PYRAMIDS
OF THE QUEENS

Below: The monument of Khentkaues I, ancestress of the Fifth Dynasty, is of a very odd form, with a rock-cut lower section and masonry upper part – not quite a mastaba, and not quite a pyramid!

Very little is known of the tombs of royal wives prior to the beginning of the Fourth Dynasty. One, the First Dynasty Meryetneith, had a large tomb and funerary enclosure at Abydos, but this was by virtue of her having been Regent for her young son, Den. Another, Neithhotep, probably the mother of Aha, had a panelled mastaba at Naqada, while Herneith, perhaps a wife of Den, was in all likelihood the owner of a tomb at Saqqara (S3507).

On this basis, it may well be that during the early years of Egypt's history queens were generally buried apart from their royal spouse, following other members of the court. However, it is likely that some who predeceased their husbands shared the king's tomb, given the discovery of probably-female bejewelled human remains in the tomb of Djer.

Two Second Dynasty princesses are known to have been buried at Saqqara, with three other royal offspring of the dynasty interred across the river at Helwan, a huge necropolis of the Archaic Period. It is possible that the vast mastaba tomb KI at Beit Khallaf might be that of Queen Nymaathap, given the presence of her name on a number of seal-impressions there. The building is some 85 metres long, 45 wide and 8 high, and incorporates one of the earliest brick arches known.

However, no further queen's tomb is evident until the reign of Khufu. Tombs of other family members are present during the time of Seneferu, all being mastabas erected some distance from the Dahshur and Meidum pyramids. This general geographical separation of the king's tomb from that of others breaks down under Khufu, who created a whole series of cemeteries close to his Great Pyramid at Giza for his family and associates. The cemetery in front of the pyramid, the East Cemetery, incorporated three small pyramids, the first of a series of such monuments that stretches on into the Thirteenth Dynasty. There are many gaps in the record however, where other types of tomb were used, or no sepulchre(s) have yet been identified.

REIGN OF KHUFU: *c.* 2547–2524 BC
GIa
This is the northernmost of the small pyramids adjacent to the Great Pyramid. Its superstructure is largely ruined, and on the east side is a small chapel. The interior consists of a descending passage giving access to a vestibule, from which a right turn leads into the burial chamber, its door some distance above the floor.

The pyramid's possible attribution is based on the proximity of G7000X, a shaft tomb just north-east of the pyramid, which held the canopic chest, empty

SITE/DESIGNATION: Giza L.V; GIa+G7000X
OWNER: Hetepheres, mother of the king(?)
DIMENSIONS: Base 47.4 x 47.4 metres

Right: This plan of the southernmost of the three pyramids built by Khufu for his wives at Giza, GIc, is typical of the original layout of these monuments. However, in the Third Intermediate and Late periods, the Old Kingdom chapel (seen here in black) was greatly enlarged to form the temple of 'Isis, mistress of the Pyramids' (seen here in grey). At the same time, the pyramid itself became associated (rightly or wrongly) with Princess Henutsen.

SITE/DESIGNATION:
Giza L.VI; GIb
OWNER: Not known
DIMENSIONS: Base 49.5
x 49.5 metres

sarcophagus and funerary furniture of Hetepheres, wife of Seneferu and mother of Khufu. A recent suggestion is that these may have been 'leftovers' following the creation by Khufu of a new set of equipment for the queen in her new role as King's Mother, at the same time as he provided for her the first pyramid created for someone other than a king – GIa.

Principal Explorations

The pyramid was opened by Vyse and Perring in 1837, and further examined by Reisner in the 1920s; the shaft was discovered by Reisner in 1925.

GIb

GIb is very similar to GIa; part of the decoration of the chapel is now in Boston, USA.

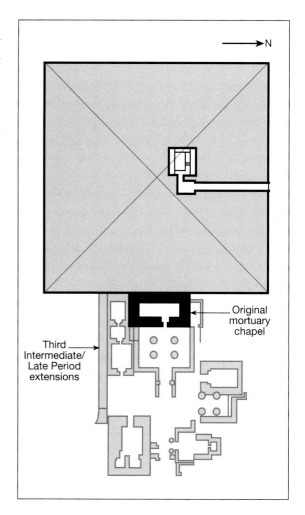

Original mortuary chapel

Third Intermediate/ Late Period extensions

Principal Explorations

Opened by Vyse and Perring in 1837, and further examined by Reisner in the 1920s.

Right: The entrance to the burial chamber of GIa is high above the floor of the chamber, an arrangement found in only a couple of pyramids of this period.

GIc

Although very similar to the monuments GIa and GIb, the pyramid of GIc is, however, much better preserved. However, during the Twenty-first Dynasty, its chapel was greatly enlarged as the temple of Isis-Mistress-of-the-Pyramids. A Twenty-sixth Dynasty stela from here attributes the pyramid to Henutsen, who is not known from any contemporary monument.

Principal Explorations

Opened by Vyse and Perring in 1837, and further examined by Reisner in the 1920s; the later temple on the east was excavated by Hassan in the 1930s.

REIGN OF DJEDEFRE: *c.* 2547–2524 BC

The pyramid lies north of the boat pit in Djedefre's complex and retains five courses of masonry just under 2 metres high. A shaft 1.5 metres deep in the middle of the north face gives access to a corridor that leads to one chamber to the east and two chambers to the west.

Objects found included some faience tiles, a calcite vessel, a dish bearing the name of Khufu, pottery fragments and two lids that might have come from canopic jars. The burial chamber contained fragments of a limestone sarcophagus.

Principal Explorations

Discovered by Valloggia in April 2002.

SITE/DESIGNATION:
Giza L.LVII; GIc
OWNER: Henutsen,
daughter of king(?)
DIMENSIONS: Base 47 x
47 metres

Above: GIc is the best preserved of the three queens' pyramids in Giza. Here, GIb reveals part of the stepped core.

SITE/DESIGNATION:
Abu Rowash
OWNER: Not Known
DIMENSIONS:
Base 12 x 12 metres

REIGN OF KHAEFRE: *c.* 2515–2493 BC

No pyramids were built for Khaefre's wives; some of these ladies, as daughters of Khufu, retained tombs in the cemetery east of the Great Pyramid, but at least two began rock-cut tombs south of Khephren's pyramid causeway at Giza. This was a considerable innovation, marking a step away from the brick- or stone-built tomb superstructures that had been standard for many years. One, lying in a former quarry south of the king's mortuary temple, belonged to Queen Persenet (LG88). The other, the 'Galarza Tomb', lay close to the bottom of the causeway of the king's pyramid, and was apparently begun for Khamerernebty I, but substantially modified by her daughter, Khamerernebty II, wife of Menkaure; the changes are believed to have had a major influence in the subsequent evolution of the rock-cut tomb at Giza.

REIGN OF MENKAURE: *c.* 2493–2475 BC

At least one of the king's spouses, Khamerernebty II, was an owner of the 'Galarza' rock-cut tomb at Giza. However, the royal complex incorporated two 'family' pyramids, in addition to the king's own subsidiary pyramid (GIIIc).

GIIIa *For plan, see page 63.*

This pyramid is well preserved; a large mud-brick chapel was constructed on the east side, on foundations intended for a stone structure. The passage into the sub-

Below: The eastern two pyramids of the three that lie south of Menkaure's monument in Giza were, after the pyramids of the queens of Khufu, the next monuments to be associated with a king's queens.

SITE/DESIGNATION:
Giza GIIIa; L.XII
OWNER: Not known
DIMENSIONS: Base 44.4
x 44.4 metres

structure was blocked by a granite portcullis, beyond which a short corridor led into the burial chamber; a sarcophagus was sunk into the floor.

GIIIb *For plan, see page 63.*

This pyramid, which has the appearance of a stepped structure, likewise has a brick chapel, its walls plastered and whitewashed. The substructure is unusual in that its entrance lies well beyond the perimeter of the pyramid, while the chambers are far to the north of its centre. This may imply that the pyramid was originally planned to lie to the north of its final location, perhaps before the king's pyramid was enlarged (see page 63). The chambers revive the practice of Khufu's time by having a right-angled turn into the burial chamber. The latter contained a granite sarcophagus, with the skeleton of a young woman.

Principal Explorations
Opened by Vyse and Perring in 1837, and re-examined by Reisner in 1906–10.

REIGN OF SHEPSESKAF (?): *c.* 2475–2471 BC

Built just north of the valley building of Menkaure, this monument comprised a square structure atop a rock-cut podium in which were excavated a chapel with inscribed door-jambs and, below the chapel, a burial chamber. It seems likely that the 'podium' was intended as a simple mastaba, albeit mainly cut from the living rock, and given inscribed panelling reminiscent of that found on tombs of the Archaic Period. The chapel and burial chamber arrangements were elaborations of the corresponding rock-cut features of late Fourth Dynasty royal family members' tombs.

Principal Explorations
The tomb was excavated by Hassan in 1932.

Right: The plan of the tomb of Khentkaues I, believed to be the mother of two kings, shows the chapel cut in the base of the super-structure, and the elaborate burial chamber below.

SITE/DESIGNATION:
Giza GIIIb; L.XI
OWNER: A young woman
DIMENSIONS: Base 31.5 x 31.5 metres

SITE/DESIGNATION:
Giza GIV; LG100;
Fourth Pyramid
OWNER: Khentkaues I, mother of two kings (?)
DIMENSIONS: Base 45.8 x 43.7 metres

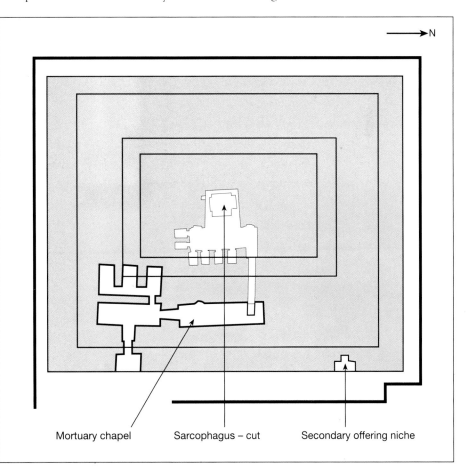

N

Mortuary chapel   Sarcophagus – cut   Secondary offering niche

SITE/DESIGNATION:
Saqqara
OWNER: Neferhetepes,
Userkaf's mother (?)
DIMENSIONS:
Base 26 x 26 metres

Right: The queen's pyramid associated with the sepulchre of Userkaf, seen here across the ruins of his mortuary temple, has lost much of its upper part, leaving the substructure open to the elements (see page 21).

REIGN OF USERKAF: *c. 2471–2464* BC

The pyramid lies south-east of the king's, and is badly ruined, with the gable-roofed burial chamber exposed and partly destroyed. The chapel was considerably more elaborate than those of earlier queens' pyramids, with a triple set of the niches that had appeared in Khentkaues I's chapel, and these would appear in most subsequent queens' offering places.

Principal Explorations

Excavated by Firth in 1928–9; work was continued between 1948 and 1955 by Lauer, who returned for further work with Labrousse in 1976–8.

SITE/DESIGNATION:
Abusir
OWNER: Khentkaues II,
Neferirkare's wife
DIMENSIONS: Base 26 x
26 metres

REIGN OF NEFERIRKARE: *c. 2452–2442* BC

The area south of the mortuary temple of Neferirkare included the pyramids of three queens. One belonged to his own reign, and was that of his wife, Khentkaues II. Its chapel was later enlarged, apparently to serve, in addition, the cult of Khentkaues I, the dynasty's ancestress. The pyramid itself is of standard form and badly ruined, containing a few fragments of the queen's sarcophagus.

Principal Explorations

Excavated by Verner in 1976–86.

Left: At Abusir, the chapel of the pyramid of Khentkaues II, wife of Neferirkare, was greatly enlarged, apparently to accommodate the cult of Khentkaues I. The queen's pyramid is in a poor state.

REIGN OF NIUSERRE:
c. 2432–2421 BC

L.XXIV

A ruined monument of the standard plan of its time, the pyramid displays interesting examples of builders' marks, shown where the facing masonry has been destroyed. The remains of a sarcophagus and parts of the mummy of a young woman were found within.

Above: Fragments of the sarcophagus of a young woman from Niuserre's reign lie in the burial chamber of *L.XXIV*; the lugs on this end of the lid were intended to make it more manoeuvrable.

Principal Explorations
Excavated by Verner in 1994–6.

L.XXV

Of similar size and form to L.XXI, little is yet known of this ruined monument.

Principal Explorations
To be excavated by Czech Archaeological Mission.

SITE/DESIGNATION: Abusir L.XXIV; J
OWNER: Not known
DIMENSIONS: Base 26 x 26 metres

REIGN OF MENKAUHOR: c. 2421–2413 BC

Since the king's probable pyramid complex has never been cleared, nothing is known of any adjacent queenly pyramid(s). However, a likely wife of the king, Meresankh IV, was buried in a mastaba (Tomb 82) some 600 metres to the south-west, close to the north wall of Djoser's enclosure.

SITE/DESIGNATION: Abusir L.XXV
OWNER: Not known
DIMENSIONS: Not known

REIGN OF ISESI: c. 2413–2385 BC

L.XXXVIII *For plan, see page 72.*

Lying north of the king's pyramid temple, this structure has one of the most elaborate mortuary chapels known for a queenly monument; however, it is badly ruined.

Principal Explorations
Noted by Perring and Lepsius in the 19th century; partly excavated by Fakhry in 1952, and surveyed by Maragioglio and Rinaldi in the 1960s.

SITE/DESIGNATION: Saqqara-South L.XXXVIII
OWNER: Not known
DIMENSIONS: Base 26 x 26 metres

REIGN OF UNAS: c. 2385–2355 BC

For plan, see page 73.

Neither of the king's wives had a pyramid. Instead, Nebet and Khenut occupied a large double mastaba north-east of the royal mortuary temple. This area also held the tombs of a number of royal offspring.

REIGN OF TETI: *c.* 2355–2343 BC

For plans, see page 74.

The tombs of the wives of Teti seem initially to have been designed as mastabas, although they ultimately took the form of pyramids. The shaft-based substructure of Iput I's original mastaba was retained after the conversion, the mouth of the shaft being covered by the pyramid, which was thus built after Iput's death. The pyramid's core was later dug out to be the chapel of a New Kingdom sepulchre.

SITE/DESIGNATION:
Saqqara
OWNER: Iput I
DIMENSIONS: Base 21 x 21 metres

The chapel has a plan that, while reminiscent of earlier examples, has certain unique features. The burial chamber contained the sarcophagus of the queen, together with her canopic jars. Although the tomb had been robbed, Iput's skeleton was found in the burial chamber.

Principal Explorations

Discovered by Loret in 1897–9 and further excavated by Firth in 1920–22 and Hawass in 1992–3.

SITE/DESIGNATION:
Saqqara
OWNER: Khuit
DIMENSIONS: Base 21 x 21 metres

The neighbouring tomb of Khuit was designed as a pyramid, and although the chapel has areas of similarity with that of Iput I, the substructure of the pyramid is in complete contrast, being of conventional form, and a miniature version of the pyramid of Teti himself. The burial chamber contained a sarcophagus, a cavity for the canopic chest and the remains of a later mummy.

Some traces to the south of the pyramids of Iput and Khuit may represent a mastaba of a third wife of Teti, but this remains uncertain.

Right: The wives of Teti were buried in this area, north-east of the king's pyramid.

Below: The double mastaba that accommodated the wives of Unas: Khenut and Nebet.

Principal Explorations

The chapel of the complex was excavated by Loret in 1897–9, and by Firth in 1922; the pyramid itself was found by Hawass in 1996–8.

REIGN OF PEPY I: *c. 2343–2297* BC

A group of six queenly pyramids lies close to the south-west corner of Pepy I's complex; at least four, probably five, of them belong to spouses of that king. Their plans all vary somewhat, although most seem to have chapels reminiscent of the previous reign, while the entrance to that of Inti was flanked by obelisks. The pyramids' interiors also vary in the orientation of their store-room and the portcullis arrangements. All were plain apart from the pyramid of Ankhenespepy II, which was adorned with Pyramid Texts, their first appearance in a queenly tomb.

Principal Explorations

Discovered and excavated by the French Mission to Saqqara from 1988 onwards. It is very possible that other queens' pyramids may yet be found in the area.

Below: The queens' cemetery south-west of Pepy I's Pyramid.

SITE/DESIGNATION: Saqqara-South
OWNER: Ankhenespepy II, wife of the king and also of Nemtyemsaf I
DIMENSIONS: Not available

SITE/DESIGNATION: Saqqara-South
OWNER: Nebwenet, wife of the king
DIMENSIONS: Base 22 x 22 metres

SITE/DESIGNATION: Saqqara-South
OWNER: Inenek-Inti, wife of the king
DIMENSIONS: Base 24 x 24 metres

SITE/DESIGNATION: Saqqara-South
OWNER: Meryetyotes IV, wife of the king
DIMENSIONS: Not available

SITE/DESIGNATION: Saqqara-South, 'Western Pyramid'
OWNER: Probably a wife of the king
DIMENSIONS: Not available

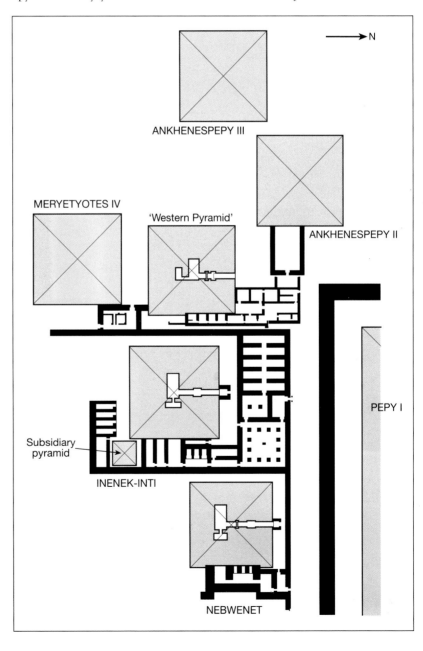

ANKHENESPEPY III

MERYETYOTES IV

'Western Pyramid'

ANKHENESPEPY II

Subsidiary pyramid

INENEK-INTI

PEPY I

NEBWENET

N

REIGN OF NEMTYEMSAF I: *c.* 2297–2290 BC

The only tomb known to belong to a spouse of Nemtyemsaf I is that of Ankhenespepy II, who had previously been married to Nemtyemsaf's father, Pepy I, and was buried in Pepy I's complex. No other wives are recorded, but a map drawn by the Prussian expedition to Egypt in the 1840s shows three approximately square mounds around the king's pyramid. Two of these are the right size for queens' pyramids, and moreover lie in almost the same position relative to the king's monument as do the tombs of Teti's queens to his.

REIGN OF PEPY II: *c.* 2290–2196 BC

One of the wives of Pepy II, Ankhenespepy III, was buried in the complex of Pepy II's father, Pepy I. Such a burial away from a husband (who had his pyramid 1.5 kilometres to the south-west) is very unusual; it is possible that this may represent the reuse of an earlier monument following Ankhenespepy's premature death.

Principal Explorations
Excavated by the French Mission in the late 1990s.

Three queens' pyramids lie adjacent to the complex of Pepy II itself. Each monument had steeply angled sides, substructures decorated with Pyramid Texts and large decorated chapels, including subsidiary pyramids. Between the subsidiary pyramid of Neith and her main pyramid, 16 wooden model ships were found. Iput's chapel had its entrance flanked by obelisks, and has the additional interest of, in later times, being used as the tomb of a queen. One of the store-rooms of one of the pyramids had a funerary stela carved into one of its walls, and a sarcophagus placed in the chamber for the burial of another wife of Pepy II, Ankhenespepy IV.

Principal Explorations
Excavated by Jéquier in the late 1920s.

Right: Plan of Iput II's complex, representing the final development of a queen's pyramid. The westernmost of the store-rooms on the south side of the monument housed the sarcophagus of Queen Ankhenespepy IV.

SITE/DESIGNATION: Saqqara-South
OWNER: Ankhenespepy III, wife of Pepy II
DIMENSIONS: Not available

SITE/DESIGNATION: Saqqara-South L.XLII
OWNER: Wedjebten, wife of the king
DIMENSIONS: Base 23.9 x 23.9 metres
For plan, see page 77.

SITE/DESIGNATION: Saqqara-South
OWNER: Iput II, wife of the king
DIMENSIONS: Base 22 x 22 metres

SITE/DESIGNATION: Saqqara-South
OWNER: Neith, wife of the king
DIMENSIONS: Base 24 x 24 metres
For plan, see page 77

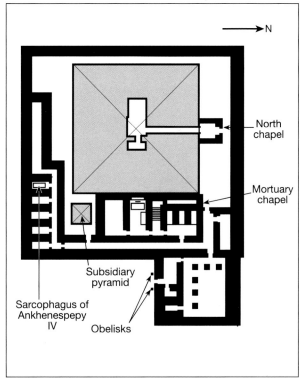

N

North chapel

Mortuary chapel

Subsidiary pyramid

Sarcophagus of Ankhenespepy IV

Obelisks

REIGN OF MONTJUHOTPE II: *c. 2066–2014* BC

After Pepy II's reign, tombs of royal family members are almost unknown from the Sixth to the Tenth dynasty. The next royal wives' sepulchres are to be found during the Eleventh Dynasty but, like those of the kings, they do not take the form of pyramids. In the saff tombs, they take the same chapel/shaft form as those of their husbands. At Deir el-Bahari, within the royal mortuary temple, a number of Montjuhotpe II's spouses had small, cupboard-like, free-standing decorated stone chapels with a shaft and burial chamber behind. One wife had a burial chamber at the end of a sloping passage close to that of the king himself.

REIGN OF AMENMEHAT I: *c. 1994–1964* BC

The resurrection of the kingly pyramid under the Twelfth Dynasty was not initially accompanied by pyramids for queens. Amenemhat I's complex (see page 85) incorporated only mastabas for his court, including, north of the mortuary temple, two mastabas (945 and 946). These were located in a similar place to the position of royal family tombs in many of the complexes of the late Old Kingdom and also in the slightly later pyramid complex of Senwosret I. South of the mortuary temple lie two large tombs, the southern of which (493) has its own enclosure, approached by a ramp from a lower level, with a massif (possibly a small pyramid) fronted by a chapel. Its position and form seem appropriate to a wife (or conceivably the mother) of the king.

Left: Iput II's Pyramid and chapel, with the false door still in position.

Above: The granite gateway of Iput II's complex.

Below: A number of the tombs of Montjuhotpe II's wives at Deir el-Bahari contained exquisite sarcophagi; this one, now in the Cairo Museum, belonged to Kawit.

Right: The pyramid complex of Senwosret I, as seen from the south-east, and the location of the pyramid of Neferu III, mother of Senwosret I, of which just a vague undulation in the sand remains. In the distance the pyramid of Amenemhat I may be seen.

SITE/DESIGNATION:
Lisht 1
OWNER: Neferu III, mother of the king
DIMENSIONS: Base 21 x 21 metres

SITE/DESIGNATION:
Lisht 2
OWNER: Itakayet, a daughter of the king
DIMENSIONS: Base 16.8 x 16.8 metres

SITE/DESIGNATION:
Lisht 3
OWNER: A daughter of the king?
DIMENSIONS: Base 16.8 x 16.8 metres

SITE/DESIGNATION:
Lisht 4
OWNER: A daughter or wife of the king?
DIMENSIONS: Base 16.8 x 16.8 metres

REIGN OF SENWOSRET I: *c.* 1974–1929 BC

Lisht 1 *For plans, see page 87.*

Under Senwosret I, the king's family were once more granted pyramidal monuments, which then continued to be used for many queens into the Thirteenth Dynasty. Nine small pyramids lie outside Senwosret's inner enclosure wall, the first of which has been assigned to Neferu on the basis of inscribed fragments found near the south-east corner of its enclosure. Neferu's pyramid was entered from a deep shaft in the middle of the north face, directly in front of an extension of the pyramid casing, against which a chapel formerly abutted. From the bottom of the shaft a passage leads to an antechamber, in the floor of which is sunk the entrance to the burial chamber, with a niche at its end.

Lisht 2 and 3

Itakayet's structure had a chapel that contained a number of 32-sided columns and decoration including offering-lists and -bearers, mortuary rituals, birds in the marshes and the tomb-owner seated before an offering-table. The substructure is of an elaborate form that is also found in the adjacent Pyramid 3. This form involved employing both an entrance shaft and a 'construction' one, covered over by the erection of the chapel against the north face of the pyramid. In Pyramid 2, the burial chamber was little more than an extension of the corridor, with a canopic niche in the left-hand wall, but in Pyramid 3, two sets of sliding stone doors were incorporated to block access, and a quartzite sarcophagus and canopic chest were placed in the chamber. Fragments of bone were found in the chamber, and a piece of a female statue was found in the chapel, but nothing is known of the owner of the pyramid.

Lisht 4

Four more small pyramids stood on the west and north sides of the king's pyramid. Pyramid 4 had two discrete sets of corridors and chambers, approached by separate shafts. The shaft in the north-east corner gave access to two levels of chambers, the upper of which had had an additional burial place and sarcophagus inserted just outside the main burial chamber. The burial chamber was so small that it could not have contained anything more than a wooden coffin and canopic chest.

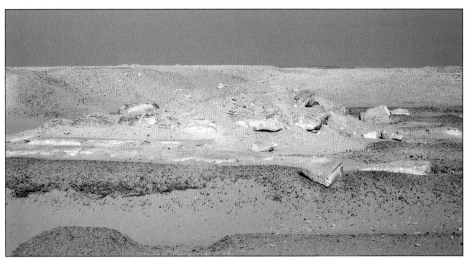

Left: Pyramid 5 in *Senwosret I's complex.*

SITE/DESIGNATION:
Lisht 5
OWNER: A daughter or wife of the king?
DIMENSIONS: Base 16.3 x 16.3 metres

SITE/DESIGNATION:
Lisht 6
OWNER: A daughter or wife of the king?
DIMENSIONS: Base 17.5 x 17.5 metres

SITE/DESIGNATION:
Lisht 7
OWNER: A daughter or wife of the king?
DIMENSIONS: Base 15.75 x 15.75 metres

SITE/DESIGNATION:
Lisht 8
OWNER: A wife of the king?
DIMENSIONS: Base 15.75 x 15.75 metres

SITE/DESIGNATION:
Lisht 9
OWNER: A wife or daughter of the king?
DIMENSIONS: Base 15.75 x 15.75 metres

Lisht 5

Although a number of tomb shafts lie around this pyramid, none leads to a conventional pyramid substructure. A shaft on the north side was unfinished, and another, on the west side, has corridors (on two levels) leading under the pyramid. These corridors, however, are collapsed and the burial chamber has never been reached.

Lisht 6 and 7

These two pyramids seem to have been built as a co-ordinated pair, and were begun around Year 13 of Senwosret I. The chapel of Pyramid 6 contained the remains of larger-than-life statues of the anonymous owner. The substructure of Pyramid 6 has not been identified, while the sloping corridor at the bottom of Pyramid 7's entrance shaft was choked with mud and never fully excavated as the water table lay just below.

Lisht 8 and 9

These two pyramids directly north of Senwosret's mortuary temple would appear to be candidates for containing queenly burials. Their dual nature, with a common enclosure wall, is reminiscent of the tombs of Nebet and Khenut, in Unas' complex, not to mention Tombs 945 and 946 in that of Amenemhat I.

Pyramid 8's chapels have disappeared, but the substructure was entered via a shaft on the centre of the north side, from the bottom of which a passageway led to a chamber under the centre of the pyramid, with a coffin-cut in the middle of the floor, and another room beyond. The adjacent Pyramid 9 had a core of brick, an unusual feature which, together with the evidence of the pottery found in its foundation deposits, suggests that it may have been built during the reigns of Amenemhat II or Senwosret II, presumably for a wife or daughter of Senwosret I who had lived into one of these reigns. The location of the substructure is uncertain, since none of the shafts in the vicinity lead to rooms that obviously relate to the pyramid.

Principal Explorations

All these sites were excavated by the Metropolitan Museum of Art between 1923 and 1933; Pyramids 1, 2, 4 and 8 had previously been investigated by Jéquier and Gautier in 1895–6.

REIGN OF AMENEMHAT II: *c.* 1932–1896 BC

Amenemhat II's complex does not seem to have incorporated pyramids for his wives, although the present state of the site may skew our perception of the situation. The two large stone and brick massifs on either side of the entry from the causeway are of uncertain purpose, but if they are tombs, their prominent position might argue for their being those of queens. Also of uncertain nature is a structure just outside the main enclosure wall, directly north of the king's pyramid, whence were recovered the remains of columns, various reused fragments and what may be an offering table of highly unusual form. If this structure does represent a tomb, a prominent owner seems likely, perhaps a queen, since the northern part of the enclosure was chosen in the next reign for the wife's probable tomb.

The one wife's burial which was recorded is in a novel form of tomb only found in this complex. Three of these exist, comprising a built structure of masonry sunk in a pit, covered by a brick relieving arch. A passage runs the entire length of the tomb, off which two niches open, each containing a sunken sarcophagus, its lid just below the level of the floor of the passage. From the west side of each sarcophagus-cut, three low openings give access to an offering/canopic chamber, returning under the paving of the passage above. At the time of the burial, the niche was filled with stone slabs, locked in place by a vertical keystone.

With their passages filled with plug blocks, the tombs effectively became solid masses of stone; doubtless this explains the fact that two of them remained intact. The third tomb was plundered by robbers breaking through the brick vault directly above the burial chambers; in its southern sarcophagus had been interred the mummy of Queen Keminub. Curiously, the northern sarcophagus was not that of a royal lady, but apparently belonged to a high official named Amenhotep. Such tombs seem unlikely to have had a monumental superstructure, and certainly not pyramids.

Below: The burial chamber of Tomb 621 was almost certainly the substructure of the Lahun queen's pyramid.

SITE/DESIGNATION:
Lahun 621
OWNER: A wife of the king, probably Neferet II or Khnemetneferhedjet I
DIMENSIONS: Base 26.6 x 26.6 metres

REIGN OF SENWOSRET II: *c.*1900–1880 BC

For plan, see page 89.

A queen's pyramid once more appears in the complex of Senwosret II. It lies just north-east of the king's, at the head of a line of mastabas of other family members. The pyramid itself is largely destroyed. No galleries lay below: what appears to have been its substructure lay some 60 metres to the north-west, presumably reflecting the security concerns of the time. Its plan is reminiscent of a king's substructure of the late Old Kingdom, but with stairways in some passages. Its sarcophagus is interesting in being among the earliest of the Middle Kingdom to adopt the palace-façade motif.

Principal Explorations
Excavated by Petrie in 1920–21.

REIGN OF SENWOSRET III: *c.* 1900–1880 BC

For plans, see page 92.

The pyramid complex of Senwosret III has, like that at Lahun, a row of royal family tombs lying along the north side of the enclosure. In this case, however, their substructures lie below the four pyramidal superstructures, comprising four individual sepulchres joined by a single east–west gallery. The only one that revealed the name of an owner was Tomb II, which contained the bones and palace-façade ornamented sarcophagus of Queen Neferhenut. While each tomb on the gallery differs from the others in detail, all resemble the queen's in basic form: a chamber leading off the main east–west corridor, a stairway and passage sunk in the floor leading to a burial chamber with two subsidiaries. A canopic niche lies at the end of a short passage west of the stairway.

Two further likely queens' pyramids lay to the south of the king's pyramid, the westernmost belonging to Weret, mother of Senwosret III. The entrance to Weret's pyramid lay some distance to the north-east of the superstructure, the shaft joining a north–south passage halfway along its 60-metre length. To the north, the passage gave access to an antechamber, a canopic room and a burial chamber, the latter with a fine granite sarcophagus displaying a panelled lower part. This all lay under the body of the king's pyramid, some 50 metres away from the queen's own monument. Under the latter, the southern part of the passage led to a small subterranean shrine.

While relief fragments were recovered from Pyramid 7, it was not possible to 'name' it. However, it had a substructure entered once again from far outside, but with a burial chamber under the monument itself.

Principal Explorations

These monuments were first investigated by de Morgan in February–March 1894; they were re-excavated by Arnold in 1994, who discovered the burial chamber of Weret, with jewellery, in November 1994.

Below: The rock-cut mastabas on the north side of the pyramid of Senwosret II at Lahun; the queen's pyramid lies at the far end of the row.

SITE/DESIGNATION:
Dahshur L.XLVII/I
OWNER: Not known

SITE/DESIGNATION:
Dahshur L.XLVII/II
OWNER: Neferhenut, wife of the king

SITE/DESIGNATION:
Dahshur L.XLVII/III
OWNER: Not known

SITE/DESIGNATION:
Dahshur L.XLVII/IV
OWNER: Not known

SITE/DESIGNATION:
Dahshur L.XLVII/9
OWNER: Weret, mother of the king

SITE/DESIGNATION:
Dahshur L.XLVII/7
OWNER: Not known

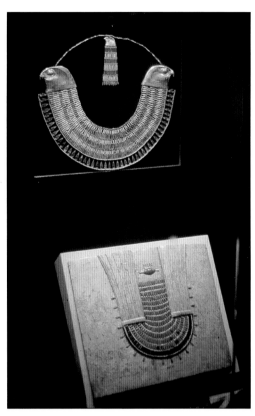

Above: The pectoral collar and restored chest area of Neferuptah's (daughter of Amenemhat III) inner coffin, now on display in the Cairo Museum.

REIGN OF AMENEMHAT III:
c. 1842–1794 BC

Amenemhat III's Black Pyramid at Dahshur further develops the arrangements of the substructure of Weret's Pyramid. Two of his wives were laid to rest wholly under his pyramid, without any separate superstructures. The queens' chambers are primarily approached via a stairway and passage from the west side of the Black Pyramid.

As we have seen above (page 96), Amenemhat III's daughter, Neferuptah, seems to have been temporarily buried in the king's burial chamber under his pyramid. She was later reburied in a pyramid two kilometres to the south, which had been designed with a burial chamber that would be roofed over and embedded in the mass of brickwork and the pyramid built over it, without any entrance passageway. This preserved the tomb intact until 1955, although the body had been destroyed by a rise in the water table. The burial chamber was divided in two by a partition wall, a huge sarcophagus lying in the southern section. The northern part held an offering table, a silver vase and a series of pots. The first two items were inscribed, as were further silver vessels from the compartment that held the sarcophagus. Another offering table and the canopics had been left behind in the main Hawara pyramid.

Principal Explorations
Noted by Habachi in 1936 and excavated by Farag and Iskander in April–May 1956.

SITE/DESIGNATION:
Hawara-South
OWNER: Neferuptah, daughter of the king
DIMENSIONS: Base 35 x 35 metres

Right: Section of the pyramid of Neferuptah, showing its lack of any entrance passage.

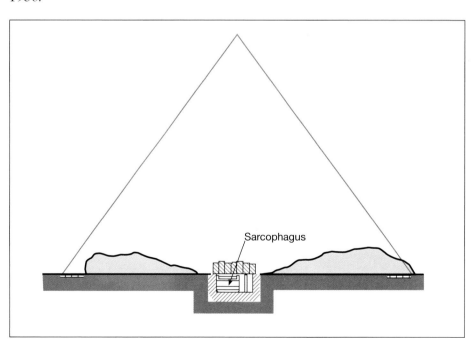

Sarcophagus

REIGN OF UNKNOWN KING: 18th century BC

For plan, see page 99.

A small pyramid was noted by Lepsius in 1843 north-east of the North Pyramid; nothing is known other than its location.

REIGN OF KHENDJER: 18th century BC

A small pyramid lay north of the site of the mortuary temple. It contains two burial chambers, reached via two portcullises; each chamber had a close-fitting sarcophagus and canopic chest. Neither chamber was ever used.

Principal Explorations
Excavated by Jéquier in 1929–31.

Later Queens' Burials

No queen's pyramid is known in Egypt subsequent to the reign of Khendjer. Indeed, very little is known of queenly interments until the Eighteenth Dynasty. Early in the Eighteenth Dynasty, a number of queens had fairly substantial rock-cut tombs of their own at Thebes, but later others seem to have been buried simply in side-rooms of kings' tombs. It was not until the Nineteenth Dynasty that a fairly consistent pattern emerges of consorts owning substantial decorated burial places in what is now known as the Valley of the Queens, where some of the royal family had been buried since the New Kingdom.

The Third Intermediate Period saw a major change in burial patterns at all levels of society, with a move towards communal burial and the large-scale abandonment of monumental chapels and burial apartments in favour of simple shaft tombs, only occasionally accompanied by modest offering places. Thus, a number of kings were accompanied by their wives in their tombs in temple courtyards. Similar, independent tombs are also found belonging to certain Third Intermediate and Late Period queens, but there are insufficient surviving examples to be able to confirm what pattern, if any, there was.

The only exception was during the Twenty-fifth Dynasty, when pyramids were re-adopted for queens' burials at El-Kurru and Nuri in the Sudan – and the queens continued, like the kings, to be interred in them following the Kushite withdrawal from Egypt. At El-Kurru, Piye's wife, Kheñsa, was buried in Ku4 and Tabiry in Ku53; adjacent were four other similar tombs, one belonging to Neferukakashta (Ku52).

Three other definite royal ladies' tombs have been identified at El-Kurru. Qalhata's Ku5 and Abar's Ku6 are some way south-east of the pyramid of Shabataka (Ku18), while the third, Ku3, of Ñaparaye, is interesting in that her husband, Taharqa, was not buried in the same cemetery, but at Nuri. On the other hand, another wife, Atakhebasken, was buried in Nuri (Nu36), where many of the subsequent queens' pyramids were erected.

SITE/DESIGNATION: Mazghuna
OWNER: Not known
DIMENSIONS: Not known

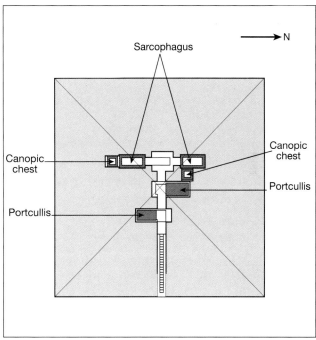

SITE/DESIGNATION: Saqqara-South L.XLV
OWNER: Probably two wives of the king
DIMENSIONS: Base 25.5 x 25.5 metres

Above: Plan of the pyramid of two wives of Khendjer of the Thirteenth Dynasty.

BIBLIOGRAPHY

ALDRED, C. 1949. *Old Kingdom Art in Egypt* (London: Tirani).

ARNOLD, Di. 1974–81. *Der Tempel des Königs Montjuhotpe von Deir el-Bahari*, 3vv (Mainz: Philipp von Zabern).

- 1976. *Gräber des Alten und Mittleren Reiches in El-Tarif* (Mainz: Philipp von Zabern).

- 1979a. *The Temple of Mentuhotep at Deir el-Bahri* (New York: MMA).

- 1979b. 'Das Labyrinth und seine Vorbilder'. *MDAIK* 35: 1–9.

- 1987. *Der Pyramidbezirk des Königs Amenemhet III in Dahschur* I: *Die Pyramide* (Mainz: Philipp von Zabern).

- 1988. *The Pyramid of Senwosret I* (New York: Metropolitan Museum of Art).

- 1991. *Building in Egypt: Pharaonic Stone Masonry* (New York: Oxford University Press).

- 1992. *The Pyramid Complex of Senwosret I* (New York: MMA).

- 1998. 'Royal Cult Complexes of the Old and Middle Kingdoms', *TAE*: 86–126.

- 2002. *The Encyclopedia of Ancient Egyptian Architecture* (London: I.B. Tauris).

ARNOLD, Di. and A. OPPEN HEIM 1995. 'Reexcavating the Senwosret III Pyramid Complex at Dahshur', *KMT* 6/2: 44–56.

ARNOLD, Di. and R. STADELMANN 1975. 'Dahschur: Grabungsberichte', *MDAIK* 31: 169–174.

ARNOLD, Do. 1991. 'Amenemhat I and the early Twelfth Dynasty at Thebes', *MMJ* 26: 5–48.

AYRTON, E., C.T. CURRELLY and A.E.P. WEIGALL 1904. *Abydos III* (London: EEF).

BADAWY, A. 1954–68. *A History of Egyptian Architecture*, 3vv. (Cairo; Berkeley: University of California Press).

BAINES, J. and J. MÁLEK 1980. *Atlas of Ancient Egypt* (New York and Oxford: Facts on File).

BARSANTI, A. 1902–12. 'Fouilles de Zaouiét el-Aryân', *ASAE* 7: 257–86; 8: 201–10; 12: 57–63.

BAUD, M. 1997. 'Aux pieds de Djoser: les mastabas entre fosse et enceinte de la partie nord du complexe funéraire', *Études Lauer*: 69–87.

BELZONI, G. 1820. *Narrative of the Operations and Recent Discoveries in Egypt and Nubia* (London: John Murray).

BERLANDINI, J. 1979. 'La pyramide "ruinée" de Sakkara-nord et le roi Ikaouhor-Menkaouhor', *RdE* 31: 3–28.

BORCHARDT, L. 1907. *Das Grabdenkmal des Königs Ne-user-reʿ* (Leipzig: Heinrichs').

- 1909. *Das Grabdenkmal des Königs Nefer-ir-ka-reʿ* (Leipzig: Heinrichs').

- 1910–13. *Das Grabdenkmal des Königs Sʾa3hu-reʿ*, 2vv (Leipzig: Heinrichs').

BOURRIAU, J.D. 1988. *Pharaohs and Mortals: Egyptian art in the Middle Kingdom* (Cambridge: University Press).

BRUNTON, G. 1920. *Lahun* I: *The Treasure* (London: BSAE).

CARTER, H. 1901. 'Report on the tomb of Mentuhotep Iˢᵗ at Deir el-Bahari, known as Bab el-Hoçan', *ASAE* 2: 201–205.

COTTRELL, L. 1956. *The Mountains of Pharaoh* (London: Robert Hale).

DAVID, R. 1986. *The Pyramid Builders of Ancient Egypt* (London: Routledge & Kegan Paul).

DAWSON, W.R., E.P. UPHILL and M.L. BIERBRIER 1995. *Who Was Who in Egyptology,* 3rd edition (London: EES).

DE MORGAN, J. 1895, 1903. *Fouilles à Dahchour* I, II (Vienna: Adolphe Holzhausen).

- 1997. *Mémoirs de Jacques de Morgan* (Paris and Montreal: L'Harmattan).

DODSON, A.M. 1987. 'The Tombs of the Kings of the Thirteenth Dynasty in the Memphite Necropolis', *ZÄS* 114: 36–45.

- 1988a. 'The Tombs of the Queens of the Middle Kingdom', *ZÄS* 115: 123–36.

- 1988b. 'Egypt's first antiquarians?'. *Antiquity* 62/236: 513–17.

- 1994. *The Canopic Equipment of the Kings of Egypt* (London: Kegan Paul International).

- 1996. 'Mysterious Second Dynasty', *KMT* 7/2: 19–31.

- 1997. 'The Strange Affair of Dr Muses', *KMT* 8/3: 60–63.

- 1998. 'On The Threshold of Glory: The Third Dynasty', *KMT* 9/2: 26–40.

- 2000a. *After the Pyramids* (London: Rubicon).

- 2000b. 'The Layer Pyramid at Zawiyet el-Aryan: Its Layout and Context', *JARCE* 38: 81–90.

DODSON, A.M. and D.L. HILTON 2004. *The Royal Family in Ancient Egypt: a genealogical sourcebook* (London: Thames and Hudson).

DODSON, A.M. and S. IKRAM 2005. *The Tomb in Ancient Egypt* (London: Thames and Hudson).

DONADONI ROVERI, A.M. 1969. *I sarcophagi egizi dalle origini alla fine dell'Antico Regno* (Rome: Università degli Studi di Roma).

DREYER, G. and N. SWELIM 1982. 'Die kleine Stufen-pyra mide von Abydos-Süd (Sinki)', *MDAIK* 38: 83–95.

DUNHAM, D. 1950. *El-Kurru* (Boston: MFA).

- 1955. *Nuri* (Boston: MFA).

- 1958. *Royal Tombs at Meroe and Barkal* (Boston: MFA).

- 1963. *The West and South Ceme teries at Meroe* (Boston: MFA).

DUNHAM, D. and S.E. CHAP MAN 1952. *Decorated Chapels of the Meroitic Pyramids at Meroe and Barkal* (Boston: MFA).

EDWARDS, I.E.S. 1947/85. *The Pyramids of Egypt* (3rd edition) (Harmondsworth: Penguin).

- 1965. 'Lord Dufferin's Excavations at Deir el-Bahri and the Clandeboye Collection', *JEA* 51: 16–28.

- 1994. 'Do the Pyramid Texts suggest an explanation for the abandonment of the subter ranean chamber of the Great Pyramid?', *Hommages Leclant*, I: 161–7.

- 1997. 'The Pyramid of Seila and its Place in the Succession of Snofru's Pyramids', in E. Goring, N. Reeves and J. Ruffle (eds.), *Chief of Seers: Egyptian Studies in Memory of Cyril Aldred* (London: Kegan Paul International): 88–96.

EL-KHOULI, A. 1991. *Meidum*

(Sydney: Australian Centre for Egyptology).

EMERY, W.B. 1961. *Archaic Egypt* (Harmondsworth: Penguin).

FAKHRY, A. 1959–61. *The Monuments of Snefru at Dahshur*, 2vv (Cairo: General Organisation for Government Printing Offices).

- 1961/72. *The Pyramids*, 2nd edition (Chicago: University Press).

FARAG, N. and Z. ISKANDER 1971. *The Discovery of Neferwptah* (Cairo: General Organization for Government Printing Offices).

FAULKNER, R.O. 1969. *The Ancient Egyptian Pyramid Texts* (Oxford: Griffith Institute).

FIRTH, C.M. and J.E. QUIBELL 1935. *The Step Pyramid* (Cairo: IFAO).

GASM EL SEED, A. 1985. 'La Tombe de Tanoutamon à El Kurru (KU. 16)', *RdE* 36: 67–72.

GAUTIER, J.E. and G. JÉQUIER 1902. *Memoire sur les fouilles de Licht* (Cairo: IFAO).

GONEIM, M.Z. 1956. *The Buried Pyramid* (London: Longman, Green)/*The Lost Pyramid* (New York: Rinehart).

- 1957. *Horus Sekhemkhet: The Unfinished Step Pyramid at Saqqara*, I (Cairo: IFAO).

GREENER, L. 1966. *The Discov ery of Egypt* (London: Cassell).

GRINSELL, L. 1947. *Egyptian Pyramids* (Gloucester: John Bellows).

HARPUR, Y. 2001. *The Tombs of Nefermaat and Rahotep at Maidum: Discovery, Destruction and Reconstruction* (Oxford: Oxford Expedition to Egypt).

HARVEY, S.P 1994. 'Monuments of Ahmose at Abydos', *EgArch* 4: 3-5.

- 2001. 'Tribute To A Conquer ing King', *Archaeology* 54/4.

HASSAN, S. 1932–60. *Excavations at Gîza*, 10vv (Cairo:

HAWASS, Z. 2000. 'Recent discoveries in the pyramid complex of Teti at Saqqara', in *AS2000*: 413–444.

HAYES, W.C. 1953, 1959. *Scepter of Egypt*, I, II (Cambridge, MA: Harvard University Press).

HÖLSCHER, U. 1912. *Das Grabdenkmal des Königs Chephren* (Leipzig: Heinrichs').

HORNUNG, H. 1990. *Valley of the Kings: Horizon of Eternity* (New York: Timken).

IKRAM, S. and A.M. DODSON, 1998. *The Mummy in Ancient Egypt: Equipment for Eternity* (London and New York: Thames and Hudson; Cairo: American University in Cairo Press).

JANOSI, P. 1996. *Die Pyramidenanlagen der Königinnen: Untersuchungen zu einem Grabtyp des Alten und Mittleren Reiches* (Vienna: Akademie der Wissenschaften).

JÉQUIER, G. 1928a. *Le Mastabat Faraoun* (Cairo: IFAO).

- 1928b. *Le Pyramide d'Oudjebten* (Cairo: IFAO).

- 1929. *Tombeaux de particuliers contemporains de Pepi II* (Cairo: IFAO).

- 1933. *Les Pyramides des Reines Neit et Apouit* (Cairo: IFAO).

- 1935. *La Pyramide d'Aba* (Cairo: IFAO).

- 1936–8. *Le monument funéraire de Pepi II*, 2vv (Cairo: IFAO).

- 1938. *Deux pyramides du Moyen Empire* (Cairo: IFAO).

- 1940. *Douze ans de fouilles dans la Nécropole Memphite* (Neuchâtel: Secrétariat de l'université).

KAISER, W. and G. DREYER 1979. 'Zu den kleinen Stufenpyramiden Ober- und Mittelägyptens', *MDAIK* 36: 43–59.

KAMAL, A. 1912. 'Fouilles à Dara et à Qoçéir el-Amarna', *ASAE* 12: 128–42.

KEMP, B.J. 1966. 'Abydos and the Royal Tombs of the First Dynasty', *JEA* 52: 13–22.

- 1967. 'The Egyptian First Dynasty Royal Cemetery', *Antiquity* 41: 22–32.

LABROUSSE, A. 1994. 'Les reines de Teti, Khouit et Ipout I, recherches architecturales', *Hommages Leclant*, I: 231–44.

- 1996–2000. *L'architecture des pyramides à textes*, 2vv (Cairo: IFAO).

- 1999. *Les pyramides des reines. Une nouvelle nécropole à Saqqâra* (Paris: Hazen).

LABROUSSE, A. and J.-Ph. LAUER 2000. *Les complexes funéraires d'Ouserkaf et de Néferhétepes* (Cairo: IFAO).

LABROUSSE, A, J.-P. LAUER and J. LECLANT 1977, *Le Temple haut du complexe funéraire du roi Ounas* (Cairo: IFAO).

LABROUSSE, A. and A.M. MOUSSA 1996, *Le temple d'accueil du complexe funéraire du roi Ounas* (Cairo: IFAO).

- 2002. *La chaussée du complexe funéraire du roi Ounas* (Cairo: IFAO).

LANDUA-MACCORMACK, D. 2002. 'Evidence for XIII Dynasty Royal Mortuary Activity at South Abydos', in *53rd Annual Meeting of the American Research Center in Egypt* (Baltimore: Johns Hopkins University): 62–3.

LAUER, J.-Ph. 1936–9. *La pyramide à degrés*, I-III (Cairo: IFAO).

- 1976. *Saqqara, Royal Necropolis of Memphis* (London: Thames and Hudson).

LAUER, J.-Ph. and J. LECLANT 1972. *Le temple haut du complexe funéraire du roi Téti* (Cairo: IFAO).

LAWTON, I. and C. OGILVIE-HERALD 1999. *Giza: the Truth* (London: Virgin).

LEHNER, M. 1985. *The Pyramid Tomb of Hetep-heres and the Satellite Pyramid of Khufu* (Mainz: Philipp von Zabern).

- 1996. 'Z500 and the Layer Pyramid of Zaiyet el-Aryan', in P. Der Manuelian (ed.), *Studies in Honor of William Kelly Simpson* (Boston: MFA).

- 1997. *The Complete Pyramids* (London and New York: Thames and Hudson).

LEPSIUS, C.R. 1849–59. *Denkmaeler aus Aegypten und Aethiopien*, 6vv (Berlin/Leipzig: Nicolaische Buchandlung).

- 1897. *Denkmaeler aus Aegypten und Aethiopien, Text* (ed. E. Naville, L. Borchardt and K. Sethe) (Leipzig: J.C. Heinrichs').

LYTHGOE, A.M. 1907-8. 'Egyptian Expedition', *BMMA* 2: 163–69; 3: 183–4.

MACE, A.C. 1914. 'Excavations at the North Pyramid of Lisht', *BMMA* 9: 207-22.

- 1921-2. 'Excavations at Lisht', *BMMA* 16 Part II: 5–19; 17 Part II: 4–18.

MALEK, J. 1994. 'King Merykare and his Pyramid', in *Hommages Leclant*, I: 203–14.

MARAGIOGLIO, V. and C.A. RINALDI 1962. *Notizie sulle piramidi di Zedefrâ, Zedkarâ Isesi, Teti* (Turin: Tip. Artale).

- 1964–77, *L'architettura delle Piramidi Menfite*, II—VIII (Rapallo: Officine Grafische Canessa).

- 1968. 'Nota sulla piramide di Ameny 'Aamu', *Orientalia* NS 37: 325–38.

MOND, R. 1905. 'Report of work in the necropolis of Thebes during the winter of 1903–04', *ASAE* 6: 78–80.

MUNRO, P. 1993. *Der Unas-Friedhof Nord-West*, I (Mainz: Philipp von Zabern).

MURNANE, W.J. 1996. *The Penguin Guide to Ancient Egypt* (2nd edition) (London: Penguin).

NAVILLE, E. and H.R. HALL 1907–13. *The XIth Dynasty Temple at Deir el-Bahari*, 3vv (London: EEF).

OPPENHEIM, A, 1995. 'A First Look at Recently Discovered 12th Dynasty Royal Jewelry from Dahshur', *KMT* 6/1: 10–11.

PETRIE, W.M.F. 1883. *The Pyramids and Temples of Gizeh* (London: Field and Tuer).

- 1889. *Hawara, Biahmu and Arsinoe* (London: Field and Tuer).

- 1891. *Illahun, Kahun and Gurob. 1889–1890.* (London: David Nutt).

- 1892. *Medum* (London: D. Nutt).

- 1896. *Naqada and Ballas 1895* (London: B. Quaritch).

- 1900. *Dendereh* (London: EEF).

- 1901a. *The Royal Tombs of the Earliest Dynasties*, 2vv (London: EEF).

PETRIE, W.M.F, E. MACKAY and G. WAINWRIGHT, 1910. *Meydum and Memphis III* (London: ERA).

PETRIE, W.M.F. et al. 1912. *The Labyrinth, Gerzeh and Mazghuneh* (London: BSAE).

PETRIE, W.M.F. et al. 1923. *Lahun II* (London: BSAE).

PETRIE, W.M.F. et al. 1925. *The Tombs of the Courtiers and Oxyrhynkhos* (London: BSAE).

PIANKOFF, A. 1968. *The Pyramid of Unas* (New York: Bollingen).

PICKAVANCE, K.M. 1981. 'The Pyramids of Snofru at Dahshur: Three Seventeenth-Century Travellers', *JEA* 67: 136—42.

POCOCKE, R. 1743–5. *A Description of the East, and some other countries* (London: J. and P. Knapton, W. Innys, W. Meadows, G. Hawkins, S. Birt, T. Longman, C. Hitch, R. Dodsley, J. Nourse, and J. Rivington).

POLZ, D. 2002. '".. die Diebe konnten es nicht erreichen .." - Eine altägyptische Akte half bei der Suche nach dem Grab des Konigs Nub-Cheper-Re Intef', *Antike Welt* July 2002

- 2003a. 'Die Grabanlage des Konigs Nub-Cheper-Re Intef in Dra' Abu el-Naga - Ein Vorbericht', *MDAIK* 59.

- 2003b. 'The pyramid complex of king Nubkheperre Intef', *EgArch* 22: 12–15.

PORTER, B. and R.B. MOSS 1933–99. *Topographical Bibliography of Ancient Egyptian Hieroglyphic Texts, Reliefs and Paintings*, 8vv, VIII by J. Malek, D. Magee and E. Miles. (Oxford: Griffith Institute).

RANDALL-MACIVER, D. and A.C. MACE 1902. *El Amrah and Abydos* (London: EES).

REEVES, N. & R. WILKINSON 1996. *The Complete Valley of the Kings* (London & New York: Thames & Hudson).

REISNER, G.A. 1931. *Mycerinus: the temples of the Third Pyramid at Giza* (Cambridge MA: Harvard UP).

- 1936. *The Development of the Egyptian Tomb Down to the Accession of Cheops.* (Oxford: University Press/Cambridge, MA: Harvard University Press).

- 1942. *A History of the Giza Necropolis*, I (Cambridge, MA: Harvard University Press).

REISNER, G.A. and W.S. SMITH 1955. *A History of the Giza Necropolis*, II (Cambridge, MA: Harvard University Press).

RIDLEY, R.T. 1983. 'The Discovery of the Pyramid Texts', *ZÄS* 110: 74–80.

ROWE, A. 1931. 'Excavations of the Eckley B. Cox, Jr. Expedition at Meydum, Egypt, 1929–30, *Pannsylvania University Museum Journal* 22 (1931): 3–46.

RYHOLT, K.S.B. 1997. *The Political Situation in Egypt During the Second Intermediate Period, c.*

1800–1550 B.C. (Copenhagen: Museum Tusculanum Press).

SALEH, M. and H. SOUROUZIAN 1987. *The Egyptian Museum Cairo: Official Catalogue* (Mainz/Cairo: Philipp von Zabern).

SANDYS, G. 1673. *The relation of a Journey begun in An. Dom. 1610*, 7th ed. (London: John Williams Junior, at the Crown in Little-Britain).

SHARP, D. 2001. 'German Excavators Find a Royal Tomb of the 17th Dynasty at Dra Abu el Naga', *KMT* 12/3: 8.

SILOTTI, A. 1996. *Guide to the Valley of the Kings* (London: Wiedenfield and Nicholson).

- 1997. *The Pyramids* (London: Weidenfield and Nicholson).

SMITH, W.S. 1949. *History of Egyptian Sculpture and Painting in the Old Kingdom*2 (Oxford: University Press).

- 1981. *The Art and Architecture of Ancient Egypt*, rev. W.K. Simpson (Harmondsworth: Penguin)

SPENCER, A.J. 1979. *Brick Architecture in Ancient Egypt* (Warminster: Aris and Phillips).

- 1982. *Death in Ancient Egypt* (Harmondsworth: Penguin).

- 1993. *Early Egypt: the Rise of Civilisation in the Nile Valley* (London: BMP).

STADELMANN, R. 1991. *Die ägyptischen Pyramiden* (Mainz: Philipp von Zabern).

STADELMANN, R. et al. 1982–3. 'Die Pyramiden des Snofru in Dahshur', *MDAIK* 38: 379–93; 39: 228–9.

- 1993. 'Pyramiden und nekropole des Snofru in Dahshur', *MDAIK* 49: 259–94.

STIÉNON, J. 1950. 'El Kôlah: Mission de la Fondation Égyptologique Reine Élisabeth, 1949', *CdE* 49: 43–5.

STROUHAL, E., V. ČERNY and L. VYHNÁNEK 2000. 'An X-ray examination of the mummy found in pyramid Lepsius No. XXIV' *AS2000*: 543–50.

STROUHAL, E. and M.F. GABALLAH 1993. 'King Djedkare Isesi and his Daughters', in W.V. Davis and R. Walker (eds.), *Biological Anthropology and the Study of Ancient Egypt* (London: BMP): 104–18.

STROUHAL, E. and L. VYHNÁNEK 2000. 'The identification of the remains of King Neferefra found in his pyramid at Abusir' *AS2000*: 551–60.

SWELIM, N. 1983. *Some Problems on the History of the Third Dynasty* (Alexandria: The Archaeological Society of Alexandria).

- 1987. *The Brick Pyramid at Abu Rowash, Number 'I' by Lepsius: a preliminary study* (Alexandria: The Archaeological Society of Alexandria).

- 1994. 'Pyramid Research from the Archaic to the Second Intermediate Period: Lists, catalogues and Objectives', in *Hommages Leclant*, I: 337–49

SWELIM, N. and A. DODSON 1998. 'On the Pyramid of Ameny-Qemau and its Canopic Equipment', *MDAIK* 54: 319–34.

TAYLOR, J.H. 1989. *Egyptian Coffins* (Princes Risborough: Shire Publications).

THOMAS, E. 1966. *The Royal Necropoleis of Thebes* (Princeton: privately printed).

UPHILL, E.P. 2000. *Pharaoh's Gateway to Eternity: The Hawara Labyrinth of King Amenemhat III* (London & New York: Kegan Paul International).

VALERIANI, D. 1837. *Atlante del basso ed alto Egitto* (Florence).

VALLOGGIA, M. 2001. *Au cœur d'une pyramide. Une mission archéologique en Egypte* (Lausanne: Musée romain de Lausanne-Vidy).

VERNER, M. 1982. 'Excavations at Abusir. Season 1980/1 – Preliminary Report', *ZÄS* 109: 75–8.

- 1994a. *Forgotten Pharaohs, Lost Pyramids* (Prague: Akademia/Skodaexport).

- 1994b. 'Abusir Pyramids 'Lepsius no. XXIV and no. XXV', in *Hommages Leclant*: 371–8.

- 1995. *The Pyramid Complex of the Royal Mother Khentkaus* (Prague: Universitas Carolina Pragensis/Academia).

- 2000. 'Who was Shepsekara, and when did he reign?', *AS2000*: 581–602.

- 2001. *The Pyramids: The Mystery, Culture and Science of Egypt's Great Monuments* (New York: Grove Press).

- 2002. *Abusir: The Realm of Osiris* (Cairo & New York: AUC Press).

VYSE, R.W.H. 1840–42. *Operations carried on at the Pyramids of Gizeh in 1837*, 3vv (London: James Fraser/John Weale/G.W. Nickisson).

WEGNER, J. 1996. *The Mortuary Complex of Senwosret III: A Study of Middle Kingdom State Activity and the Cult of Osiris at Abydos* (Ann Arbor: UMI).

WEILL, R., Mme TONY-REVILLON and M. PILLET 1958. *Dara: campaignes de 1946–1948* (Cairo: Organisme Générale des Imprimeries Gouvernmentales).

WILKINSON, R.H. 2000. *The Complete Temples of Ancient Egypt* (London: Thames and Hudson).

WINLOCK, H.E. 1915. 'The Theban Necropolis in the Middle Kingdom', *AJSLL* 32: 1–37.

- 1924a. 'The Tombs of the Kings of the Seventeenth Dynasty at Thebes', *JEA* 10: 217–77.

- 1942. *Excavations at Deir el Bahri* (New York: Macmillan).

- 1947 *The Rise and Fall of the Middle Kingdom in Thebes* (New York: Macmillan).

ABBREVIATIONS

AJSLL –*American Journal of Semitic Languages and Literatures* (Chicago)

ASAE – *Annales du Service des Antiquités de l'Égypte* (Cairo)

AS2000 – *Abusir and Saqqara in the Year 2000*, ed M. Bárta and J. Krejcí (Prague: Academy of Sciences of the Czech Republic, 2000)

AUC – American University in Cairo

BIFEAO –*Bulletin de l'Institut Français d'Archéologie Orientale du Caire* (Cairo)

BioAnth – *Biological Anthropology and the Study of Ancient Egypt* (ed. W.V.-Davies and R. Walker) (London: British Museum Press, 1993)

BM – British Museum, London

BMFA – *Bulletin of the Museum of Fine Arts* (Boston)

BMMA – *Bulletin of the Metropolitan Museum of Art* (New York)

BMP – British Museum Press

BSAA – *Bulletin Société archéologique d'Alexandrie* (Alexandria)

BSAE – British School of Archaeology in Egypt

BSFE – *Buletin de la Societé Français d'Egyptologie* (Paris)

CdE – *Chronique d'Egypte* (Brussels)

CM – Egyptian Museum, Cairo.

DE – *Discussions in Egyptology* (Oxford)

EEF/S – Egypt Exploration Fund/Society

EgArch – *Egyptian Archaeology: Bulletin of the Egypt Exploration Society* (London)

ERA – Egyptian Research Account

Études Lauer – *Études sur l'Ancien Empire et la nécropole de Saqqára dédiées à Jean-Phillipe Lauer* (ed. C. Berger and B. Mathieu) (Montpellier: Université Paiul Valéry, 1997)

GM – *Göttinger Miszellen* (Göttingen)

Hommages Leclant –C. Berger, G. Clerc and N. Grimal (eds.), *Hommages à Jean Leclant*, I (Cairo: IFAO)

IFAO – Institut Français d'Archéologie Orientale

JARCE – *Journal of the American Research Center in Egypt* (New York, &c)

JE – Journal d'Entree (CM)

JEA – *Journal of Egyptian Archaeology* (London)

JNES – *Journal of Near Eastern Studies* (Chicago)

KMT – *KMT: a Modern Journal of Ancient Egypt* (San Francisco/

Sebastopol)
KV – Prefix for tombs in Valley of the Kings
L. – Prefix for pyramids numbered by Lepsius
LÄ – *Lexikon der Ägyptologie* (Weisbaden)
LG – Prefix for tombs at Giza numbered by Lepsius
LS – Prefix for tombs at Saqqara numbered by Lepsius
MDAIK – *Mitteilungen des Deutschen Archäologischen Instituts, Kairo* (Mainz)
MFA – Museum of Fine Arts, Boston

MMA – Metropolitan Museum of Art, New York
NRT – Prefix for royal tombs at Tanis
OMRO – *Oudheidkundige Mededelingen uit het Rijksmuseum van Oudheden te Leiden* (Leiden)
P7ICE – *Proceedings of the Seventh International Congress of Egyptologists*, ed. C.J. Eyre (Leuven: Peeters, 1997)
P8ICE – *Egyptology at the Dawn of the Twenty-First Century: Proceedings of the Eighth International Congress of Egyptologists, Cairo, 2000*, ed. Z.Hawass & L.P. Brock (Cairo:

AUC Press 2001)
RdE – *Revue d'Egyptologie* (Leuven)
SAK – *Studien zur altägyptschen Kultur* (Hamburg)
SR – Special Register (CM)
Stud. Smith – A. Leahy and J. Tait (eds.), *Studies on Ancient Egypt in Honour of H.S. Smith* (London: EES, 1999)
TA – Prefix for tombs at Tell el-Amarna
TAE – B.E. Schafer (ed.), *Temples in Ancient Egypt* (London: I.B. Tauris, 1998)
TR – Temporary Register (CM)
TT – Theban Tomb: the num-

bering series used for important tombs outside the Valley of the Kings and Queens
UC – Petrie Museum, University College London
U. Reed – C. Eyre, A. Leahy and L.M. Leahy (eds.), *The Unbroken Reed: Studies in the Culture and Heritage of Ancient Egypt In Honour of A.F. Shore* (London: Egypt Exploration Society, 1994)
VA – *Varia Ægyptiaca* (San Antonio, TX)
ZÄS – *Zeitschrift für Ägyptische Sprache und Altertumskunde* (Leipzig, Berlin)

GLOSSARY

Amun(-Re)
Chief god of Thebes and paramount god of Egypt from the New Kingdom onward.

Anubis
God of embalming, represented with a jackal's head.

Apis
Sacred bull of Memphis, a form of Ptah.

Book of the Dead
One of the many funerary books containing spells that would help transport the deceased safely to the next world. Common from the New Kingdom onward.

Books of the Underworld
Compositions dating to the New Kingdom that are mainly concerned with the nocturnal journey of the Sun God through the Underworld. They include the Books of the Gates, Amduat and the Earth.

canopic
Of or pertaining to the preservation of the viscera removed from the body in the course of embalming.

coffin
A container for a body of a type usually intended to lie within a sarcophagus. It may be rectangular or anthropoid, of stone or wood, but will always have a separate lid and box/trough.

Coffin Texts
Texts inscribed on the interior of the coffin to aid the deceased in reaching the next world.

corbel-roofing
Arrangement for spanning a space by setting each successive course of the walls slightly further out than the one below until they meet at the apex.

faience
Glazed blue vitreous material made from quartz sand, soda and a copper-ore based colourant.

false door
A vertical slab of stone carved in imitation of a door, usually bearing texts referring to the provision of offerings. It normally stood in the sanctuary and was the focus of the cult of the deceased. Symbolically, it was the place where the dead and the living came together, through which the dead could emerge and partake of offerings.

Heb-sed
The jubilee festival celebrated by the Egyptian king, usually after 30 years on the throne, and then repeated every three years.

hypostyle hall
Chamber with its room supported by a number of columns.

mastaba
A tomb-type, common from the Archaic Period onward. The name, mastaba, derives from

the Arabic word for mudbrick bench, which the tombs resemble.

mummy
Artificially preserved human or animal corpse. The word is derived from the Persian 'mum', meaning wax or bitumen.

natron
Combination of sodium carbonate and sodium bicarbonate, used for dessication and purification purposes in mummification. Occurs naturally in the Wadi Natrun, some 65 kilometres north-west of Cairo, as well as in certain other locations.

Opening of the Mouth
Ceremony which served to reanimate the corpse.

Osiris
God of the Dead and resurrection, brother-husband of Isis, murdered by his brother Seth and who consequently became the first mummy.

peristyle court
Courtyard with a row of columns round its edges.

Pyramid Texts
Magical texts inscribed in the burial chambers of pyramids from the end of the Fifth Dynasty onward.

pyramidion
Cap-stone of a pyramid, often made of hardstone and bearing

inscriptions; some examples may have been gilded.

rock-cut tomb
A sepulchre whose chapel is carved out of the living rock, with minimal, if any, built structure.

sarcophagus
Rectangular/quasi-rectangular outermost container, intended to hold coffins of a different form or material. It may be composed of stone or wood.

serdab
Closed chamber containing statue(s), normally with a narrow slit or other opening leading into the offering chapel to allow the statue(s) to 'see' out and for incense to drift in.

shabti
Magical servant figure found in tombs mid-Middle Kingdom onward. From the middle of the Eighteenth Dynasty, large numbers of shabti are to be found in a single burial, ultimately exceeding 400 in certain interments.

step pyramid
Pyramid rising in a series of deep steps to the summit, perhaps symbolic of a stairway to heaven.

true pyramid
Pyramid intended to have a uniform, smooth slope to the summit, perhaps representative of the sun's descending rays and a ramp to aid the kings ascension.

CHRONOLOGY

NB: Only kings with known tombs are mentioned.

	Conjectural dates (yrs BC)	Location of tomb	Tomb designation
PREDYNASTIC PERIOD			
Badarian Culture	5000–4000		
Naqada I (Amratian) Culture	4000–3500		
Naqada II (Gerzian) Culture	3500–3150		
PROTODYNASTIC PERIOD			
Naqada III Culture	3150–3000		
ARCHAIC PERIOD			
Dynasty I	3050–2813		
Narmer		Umm el-Qaab	B17/18
Aha		Umm el-Qaab	B10/15/19
Djer		Umm el-Qaab	O
Djet		Umm el-Qaab	Z
Den		Umm el-Qaab	T
Adjib		Umm el-Qaab	X
Semerkhet		Umm el-Qaab	U
Qaa		Umm el-Qaab	Q
Dynasty II	2813–2663		
Hotepsekhemwy		Saqqara	A
Nebre		?Saqqara	
Ninetjer		Saqqara	B
Weneg		?	
Sened		?Saqqara	
Peribsen	–2680	Umm el-Qaab	P
Khasekhemwy	2690–2663	Umm el-Qaab	V
OLD KINGDOM			
Dynasty III	2663–2597		
Djoser	2663–2643	Saqqara	L.XXXII; Step Pyramid
Sanakht	2643–2633	?Abu Rowash	El-Deir
Sekhemkhet	2633–2626	Saqqara	Unfinished Pyramid
Khaba	2626–2621	Zaiwiyet el-Aryan	L.XIV; Layer Pyramid
Huni	2621–2597	?Abu Rowash	L.I; Brick Pyramid
Dynasty IV	2597–2471		
Seneferu	2597–2547	Dahshur	L.XLI; Red Pyramid
Khufu	2547–2524	Giza	L.IV; Great Pyramid
Djedefre	2524–2516	Abu Rowash	L.II
Seth?ka	2516–2515	Zawiyet el-Aryan	L.XIII; Unfinished Pyramid
Khaefre	2515–2493	Giza	L.VIII; Second Pyramid
Menkaure	2493–2475	Giza	L.IX; Third Pyramid
Shepseskaf	2475–2471	Saqqara-South	L.XLIII; Mastabat Faraun

	Conjectural dates (yrs BC)	Location of tomb	Tomb designation
Dynasty V	2471–2355		
Userkaf	2471–2464	Saqqara	L.XXXI
Sahure	2464–2452	Abusir	L.XLVIII
Neferirkare	2452–2442	Abusir	L.XXI
Shepseskare	2442–2435	Abusir	–
Neferefre	2435–2432	Abusir	L.XXVI; Unfinished Pyramid
Niuserre	2432–2421	Abusir	L.XX
Menkauhor	2421–2413	Saqqara	L.XXIX
Isesi	2413–2385	Saqqara-South	L.XXXVII
Unas	2385–2355	Saqqara	L.XXXV
Dynasty VI	2355–2195		
Teti	2355–2343	Saqqara	L.XXX
Pepy I	2343–2297	Saqqara-South	L.XXXVI
Nemtyemsaf I	2297–2290	Saqqara-South	L.XXXIX
Pepy II	2290–2196	Saqqara-South	L.XLI
FIRST INTERMEDIATE PERIOD			
Dynasty VII/ VIII	2195–2155		
Ibi	2185	Saqqara-South	L.XL
Dynasties IX/X	2160–2040		
Merykare	–2042	?Saqqara	
Dynasty XIa	2160–2066		
Inyotef I	2140–2123	El-Tarif	Saff el-Dawaba
Inyotef II	2123–2074	El-Tarif	Saff el-Qisasiya
Inyotef III	2074–2066	El-Tarif	Saff el-Baqar
MIDDLE KINGDOM			
Dynasty XIb	2080–1994		
Montjuhotpe II	2066–2014	Deir el-Bahari	XIth Dynasty Temple
Montjuhotpe III	2014–2001	?Sheikh Abd el-Qurna West	TT280
Dynasty XII	1994–1781		
Amenemhat I	1994–1964	Lisht	L.LX
Senwosret I	1974–1929	Lisht	L.LXI
Amenemhat II	1932–1896	Dahshur	L.LI; White Pyramid
Senwosret II	1900–1880	Lahun	L.LXVI
Senwosret III	1881–1840	Dahshur	L.XLVII
Amenemhat III	1842–1794	Hawara	L.LXVII; Black Pyramid
Amenemhat IV	1798–1785	?Dahshur	L.LIV
Sobkneferu	1785–1781	?Dahshur	L.LIV
Dynasty XIII	1781–1650		
Amenemhat V		?Dahshur	L.LIV
Qemau		Dahshur-South	–
Amenemhat VI		?Dahshur	L.LIV
Hor		Dahshur	L.LVIII/I
Khendjer		Saqqara-South	L.XLIV
Iy		?	

	Conjectural dates (yrs BC)	Location of tomb	Tomb designation
SECOND INTERMEDIATE PERIOD			
Dynasty XV	**1650–1535**		
Dynasty XVI	**1650–1590**		
Dynasty XVII	**1585–1549**		
Inyotef V		Dira Abu'l-Naga	
Inyotef VI		Dira Abu'l-Naga	
Sobkemsaf II		Dira Abu'l-Naga	
Taa I	–1558	Dira Abu'l-Naga	
Taa II	1558–1553	Dira Abu'l-Naga	
Kamose	1553–1549	Dira Abu'l-Naga	
NEW KINGDOM			
Dynasty XVIII	**1549–1298**		
Ahmose I	1549–1524	Abydos	
Amenhotpe I	1524–1503	?Dira Abu'l-Naga	K93.11
Thutmose I	1503–1491	Valley of Kings	KV20 & KV38
Thutmose II	1491–1479	Valley of Kings	KV42
Thutmose III	1479–1424	Valley of Kings	KV34
Hatshepsut	1472–1457	Valley of Kings	KV20
Amenhotpe II	1424–1398	Valley of Kings	KV35
Thutmose IV	1398–1388	Valley of Kings	KV43
Amenhotpe III	1388–1348	Valley of Kings	WV22
Amenhotep IV/ Akhenaten	1360–1343	Tell el-Amarna	TA26
Smenkhkare/ Neferneferuaten	1346–1343	Valley of Kings	KV55
Tutankhamun	1343–1333	Valley of Kings	KV62
Ay	1333–1328	Valley of Kings	WV23
Horemheb	1328–1298	Valley of Kings	KV57
Dynasty XIX	**1298–1187**		
Rameses I	1298–1296	Valley of Kings	KV16
Sethy I	1296–1279	Valley of Kings	KV17
Rameses II	1279–1212	Valley of Kings	KV7
Merenptah	1212–1201	Valley of Kings	KV8
Sethy II	1201–1195	Valley of Kings	KV15
Amenmesse	1200–1196	Valley of Kings	KV10
Siptah	1195–1189	Valley of Kings	KV47
Tawosret	1189–1187	Valley of Kings	KV14
Dynasty XX	**1187–1064**		
Sethnakhte	1187–1185	Valley of Kings	KV14
Rameses III	1185–1153	Valley of Kings	KV11
Rameses IV	1153–1146	Valley of Kings	KV2
Rameses V Amenhirkopshef I	1146–1141	Valley of Kings	KV9
Rameses VI Amenhirkopshef II	1141–1133	Valley of Kings	KV9
Rameses VII Itamun	1133–1125	Valley of Kings	KV1
Rameses IX Khaemwaset I	1123–1104	Valley of Kings	KV6
Rameses X Amenhirkopshef III	1104–1094	Valley of Kings	KV18
Rameses XI Khaemwaset II	1094–1064	Valley of Kings	KV4

	Conjectural dates (yrs BC)	Location of tomb	Tomb designation
THIRD INTERMEDIATE PERIOD			
Dynasty XXI	**1064–940**		
Nesibanebdjed	1064–1038	?Tanis	NRT-I
Pasebkhanu I	1034–981	Tanis	NRT-III
Amenemopet	984–974	Tanis	NRT-IV
Siamun	968–948	Tanis	NRT-III
Pasebkhanu II	945–940	Tanis	NRT-III
Dynasty XXII	**948–715**		
Osorkon II	877–838	Tanis	NRT-I
Shoshenq III	838–798	Tanis	NRT-V
Shoshenq IV	798–786	Tanis	NRT-V
Pimay	786–780	Tanis	NRT-II
Shoshenq V	780–743	Tanis	NRT-I
Dynasty XXIII	**867–724**		
Harsiese	867–857	Medinet Habu	MHI
Dynasty XXIV	**731–717**		
Dynasty XXV	**752–656**		
Pi(ankh)ye	752–717	El-Kurru	Ku17
Shabaka	717–703	El-Kurru	Ku15
Shabataka	703–690	El-Kurru	Ku18
Taharqa	690–664	Nuri	NuI
Tanutamun	664–656	El-Kurru	Ku16
SAITE PERIOD			
Dynasty XXVI	**664–525**	Sais (according to Herodotus)	
LATE PERIOD			
Dynasty XXVII	**525–405**	Nashq-i Rastam, Perseopolis, Iran	
Dynasty XXVIII	**404–399**		
Dynasty XXIX	**399–380**		
Nayfarud I	399–393	Mendes	
Dynasty XXX	**380–342**		
Dynasty XXXI	**342–332**		
HELLENISTIC PERIOD			
Dynasty of Macedonia	**332–310**		
Dynasty of Ptolemy	**310–30**	Alexandria	

ROMAN PERIOD 30 BC–AD 395
BYZANTINE PERIOD AD 395–640
ARAB PERIOD AD 640–1517
OTTOMAN PERIOD AD 1517–1805
KHEDEVAL PERIOD AD 1805–1914
BRITISH PROTECTORATE AD 1914–1922
MONARCHY AD 1922–1953
REPUBLIC AD 1953–

INDEX

Page numbers in italic refer to illustrations and captions

ACKNOWLEDGEMENTS

Picture Acknowledgements

Where approporiate, the photographer/artist (AMD: Aidan Dodson) is followed by the owner of the object and the object's museum number; for museum abbreviations see pages I38–9:
b = bottom; *c* = centre; *t* = top; *l* =left; *r* =right

Front cover: Pictures Colour Library Ltd; back cover: Pictures Colour Library Ltd; spine: James Morris/Axiom; p.2: Pictures Colour Library Ltd; p.4: AMD/CM CG14; p. 5: AMD; p.7 Dyan Hilton; pp.8–17: AMD; p.18: V. Denon, *Voyage dans la Basse et la Haute Egypte*, II (Paris, 1802), pl. 20*bis*[I]; p.19: *Illustrated London News* 1895; pp.20–23: AMD; p.24: Sandys 1673: 106; p.25 (*t*): Pococke 1743–35: pl. XVIII, (*b*): AMD; p.26 (*t*): Vyse 1840–42, (*b*): AMD; p.27 (*l*): AMD collection, (*b*): *Illustrated London News* 1895, (*r*): G. Brunton, *ASAE* 48 (1948); p.28 (*l*): AMD collection, (*r*): AMD/Louvre; p.29: AMD collection; p.30: Pictures Colour Library Ltd; p.32: Pictures Colour Library Ltd; p.33: The Ancient Egypt Picture Library; p.34 (*t*): David Moyer/BM EA32751, (*bl*): AMD/BM EA58522, (*bc*): AMD/BM EA36327, (*br*): AMD/Ashmolean Museum E 3632; p.35 (*t*): AMD, (*bl*): AMD/Louvre E11007, (*bc*): AMD/BM EA32650, (*br*): AMD/BM EA35597; pp.36–7: AMD; p.38 (*t*): AMD, (*b*) Leslie Grinsell Collection, courtesy of Bristol City Museum & Art Gallery; p.39: AMD/BM EA35597; p.40 (*t*): Pictures Colour Library Ltd:, (*bl*): AMD, (*bcl*): AMD/CM JE36143, (*bcr*): AMD/CM CG14, (*br*): AMD/CM JE–79195; p.41 (*t*): AMD, (*bl*): AMD/Louvre E3023, (*br*): AMD/CM JE65908; p.42: AMD; p.43: Girolamo Segato, from Valeriani 1837: pl.37D, colorized after Silotti 1997; pp.44–5: AMD; p.46: Royal Air Force, from Leslie Grinsell Collection, courtesy of Bristol City Museum & Art Gallery; p.47: Lepsius 1859: I, pl. 12; p.48: Tarek Swelim, courtesy of

Nabil Swelim; pp.49–51: AMD; p.52: AMD/CM JE98943; p.53: Dyan Hilton; p.54: AMD; p.55: Dennis C. Forbes; p.56: AMD; p.57 (*t*): AMD, (*b*): Leslie Grinsell, courtesy of Department of Archaeology, University of Bristol; pp.58–9: AMD; p.60 (*t*): Leslie Grinsell Collection, courtesy of Bristol City Museum & Art Gallery, (*b*): AMD; p.61: AMD; p.62: AMD/CM CG15; pp.63–6: AMD; p.67: AMD/CM JE39532; pp.68–70: AMD; p.71 (*t*): AMD/Louvre E3028, (*b*): AMD; pp.72–9: AMD; p.80: AMD (*t*): , (*bl*): AMD/BM EA720. (*bcl*): AMD/Louvre A23, (*bcr*): MMA 26.7.1394, (*br*): AMD/CM CG392; p.81 (*br*): AMD/CM CG259, (*bcl*): Leslie Grinsell, courtesy of Department of Archaeology, University of Bristol/CM JE53668, (*bcr*): AMD/CM CG42027, (*br*): AMD/Louvre E.3020 and E.3019; p.82: Leslie Grinsell, courtesy of Bristol City Museum & Art Gallery; pp.84–6: AMD; p.87: AMD/CM JE58909+58910+58914; p.88: AMD; p.90 (*t*): Petrie et al. 1923; p.91: AMD/CM CG23043; p.92: Adela Oppenheim, courtesy of the Egyptian Expedition of The Metropolitan Museum of Art, New York; p.93: Josef Wegner; p.94: AMD; p.96: AMD/CM CG42022; pp.97–101: AMD; p.102 (*t*): AMD/CM JE53045, (*b*): Leslie Grinsell, courtesy of Bristol City Museum & Art Gallery; p.104: AMD/CM TR 5/1/15/12; p.105: AMD; p.106: AMD/Brussels Royal Museum of Art & History E.6857; p.107 (*t*): AMD/BM EA478, (*b*): AMD/Louvre E3020, E3019; p.108: AMD; p.109: G. Elliot Smith, *The Royal Mummies* (Cairo, 1912); p.110: AMD; p.III: Laura Foos, courtesy of Stephen P. Harvey; pp.112–13: AMD; p.114–17: Jacke Phillips; pp.118–128: AMD; p.129 (*t*): AMD, (*b*): Leslie Grinsell, courtesy of Bristol City Museum & Art Gallery/CM 47397; pp.130–32: AMD; p.132: Petrie et al. 1923; p.133: AMD; p.134: AMD/CM JE90199, 90201/2

Author's Acknowledgements

To my wife Dyan Hilton for continuing a relationship that began against the backdrop of the pyramids; to both her and Sheila Hilton for their painstaking reading of the manuscript; to Salima Ikram for many years of companionship in and around pyramids; to Nabil Swelim, Josef Wegner, Adela Oppenheim and Dennis Forbes for the provision of photographs, and also to Nabil for many discussions regarding the pyramids and various offprints and advance copies of articles; to Miroslav Verner, Miroslav Bárta and Ladislav Bareš for many kindnesses over the years at 'their' site of Abusir, including the opportunity to climb the pyramid of Neferirkare – and get down again alive!